S
DECENCIES

Reflections
and
Meditations
on
Being Human
at Work

JOHN COWAN

HarperBusiness
A Division of HarperCollins*Publishers*

A hardcover edition of this book was published in 1992 by HarperBusiness, a division of HarperCollins Publishers.

SMALL DECENCIES. Copyright © 1992 by John Cowan. All rights reserved. Printed in the United States of America. No part of this book may be used or reproduced in any manner whatsoever without written permission except in the case of brief quotations embodied in critical articles and reviews. For information address HarperCollins Publishers, Inc., 10 East 53rd Street, New York, NY 10022.

HarperCollins books may be purchased for educational, business, or sales promotional use. For information please write: Special Markets Department, HarperCollins Publishers, Inc., 10 East 53rd Street, New York, NY 10022.

First paperback edition published 1993.

Designed by C. Linda Dingler

The Library of Congress has catalogued the hardcover edition as follows:

Cowan, John, 1935–
    Small decencies : reflections and meditations on being human at work / by John Cowan. — 1st ed.
        p.   cm.
    ISBN 0-88730-559-8 (cloth)
    1. Business ethics. 2. Management—Moral and ethical aspects.
I. Title.
HF5387.C68   1992   91-58502
650.1'3—dc20

ISBN 0-88730-636-5 (pbk.)

93 94 95 96 97 ❖/HC 10 9 8 7 6 5 4 3 2 1

SMALL
DECENCIES

To Edith,
my wife,
for being wonderful

CONTENTS

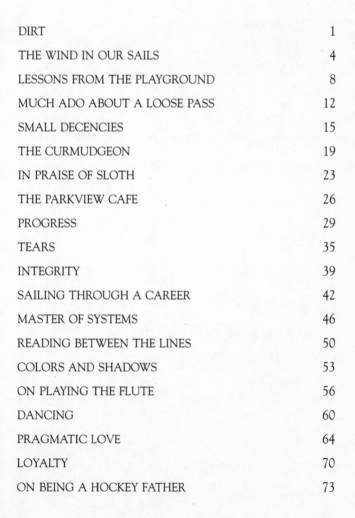

SMALL
DECENCIES

DIRT

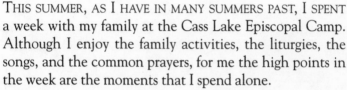

THIS SUMMER, AS I HAVE IN MANY SUMMERS PAST, I SPENT a week with my family at the Cass Lake Episcopal Camp. Although I enjoy the family activities, the liturgies, the songs, and the common prayers, for me the high points in the week are the moments that I spend alone.

I sit on a spot of dirt under a medium-sized tree, on the edge of a clearing, at the top of the hill overlooking the lake. This spot of dirt is sacred. I don't know what made it so. Perhaps it is forty years of people like me sitting on it. Perhaps the Chippewa danced here, smoked the pipe, erected the sweat lodge. I don't know who made it so, but I know that it is sacred, for after I sit here a while, I can remember who I am. And see the world for what it is.

I once asked a senior officer of a major corporation how he was responding to the devastating problems the corporation faced. "It's easy," he said, "we'll lose a couple of divisions and then we will be all right."

How many pregnant women would hear that their husbands no longer had health insurance? How many young men and women would have to change their choice of colleges? How many bicycles would not be bought for Christmas? How many families would have to try to live on a welfare check? How many single mothers would regret exchanging rent for the mortgage payment? How many men would struggle not to think of themselves as useless? How could a perfectly nice man, a well mannered gentleman, fail to factor these elements into his assessment of the situation?

I do not think that two divisions meant to him a couple of thousand people. I think that for him two divisions had become a series of numbers projected on a conference room screen. The man who saw no problem walked on concrete, drove on asphalt, flew on jets, and made his decisions on the twenty-eighth floor. It is easy to forget the dirty consequences of decisions in rooms where the windows are sealed shut, the air-conditioning runs forever, and the ground is far below. I think it was this distance that made him callous to the human effects of the corporation's financial problem and that helped cause the financial problems in the first place.

I fear being too far from the dirt. There is a G. K. Chesterton story, one of the Father Brown mysteries, about the town drunk who was struck dead by the hammer of Thor. Actually it was an ordinary hammer, but it had been swung with the violence and strength of a god, cleaving the man nearly in two. The mystery's solution is that the local vicar did it. To be closer to God, he was accustomed to praying in the bell tower. Viewing the world from that vantage point had, over the years, convinced him that he was superior to other people, that they, down there on the ground, were but a form of insect. So as he prayed, he felt no qualm about dropping a workman's hammer over the side upon the drunken beetle below.

I fear "clean." I am wary of straight ties, polished smiles, tidy rooms, immaculate résumés, and antiseptic press releases. They smell to me of artifice and danger. I never completely trust anyone until they belch, swear, weep, or bleed. If it lives, it's dirty. Clean is a cover-up.

I wish all managers had their own plot of sacred dirt. One they could sit on regularly, getting grass stains on their shorts, stray ants on their backs, and a little bark from the tree in their hair. A spot where if they sit for an hour or two, they can remember who they are and see the world for what it is.

I don't think managers and executives should avoid the hard decisions. I think the two divisions had to go. I know sometimes people must be fired. I know sometimes salaries must be frozen. I know sometimes people must be pushed to do the unpleasant task. I applaud managers who take tough steps when tough steps need to be taken. But I feel much safer if those actions are taken not by somebody who worships in the tower next to God, but by somebody who knows who he is and sees the world for what it is—someone who is accustomed to sitting in the dirt.

THE WIND IN OUR SAILS

I FIRST MET THEM AS I LEFT THE RADISSON HOTEL AFTER a filling breakfast. I was pulling on my old blue winter parka against the cold mist of an all-too-typical June morning on Lake Superior. They were comfortably encased in matching white weather gear, with the name of their boat stenciled in blue and red neatly down their sleeves.

"Chilly morning," she said, with the bemused smile those of us who patrol that lake reserve for one another.

"Going sailing?" he asked.

We chatted for a while about this and that. I learned that they had owned their boat for a couple of years. He was president of a small and thriving company. They would be sailing the harbor in deference to the wind, which was beginning to reach its forecasted strong velocity and blow away the mist. "I may see you out there," I said as I went off in pursuit of my crew, my son David.

The second time I saw them was in the channel on the way from the marina to the harbor. David had the tiller. He had seen them coming from behind and couldn't figure out how to get out of their way. I assured him that we had the right of way, even if our helmsman was eight years old and theirs was forty. I also assured him they would slow down and follow us.

My liking for them took a decided dip as they squeezed past right at the marina entrance buoy, grinning and waving happily, oblivious to the consternation they were causing the small boy at the tiller.

We were side by side as our sails popped into place. Almost simultaneously we turned off our motors, brought our sails under control, and set off on parallel paths down the harbor.

Usually I feel that any two sailboats on the same body of water makes a sailboat race, but in this case I promptly forgot about racing them. I was busy, since David finds sailing boring and had already disappeared into the cabin to do something interesting. He had left me handling the sheets with my hands, steering with my left leg over the tiller, and smoking my cigar with whatever appendages were temporarily free. Also, if I raced, I did not have a chance of winning. I based this on Cowan's second law of sailboating: "A sailboat's speed is directly related to the amount of money sunk into the boat." Since mine had cost eight thousand dollars and theirs about eighty, the result of the race was already clear.

I noticed them the third time an hour later, when David emerged from the cabin for a breath of air.

"How come they're so far back?"

"Who?"

"The other sailboat."

I turned and looked. They were about a quarter mile behind. It was a pretty picture. Their thirty-foot sloop was heeled well over on her side, carrying every ounce of sail she could carry, all sheets pulled in until the sails were completely taut, bellying in smooth and beautiful curves.

And that was why she was so far back, for what looks so lovely on calendars does not make the boat go. She was carrying too much sail for the wind, which forced her over onto her side. A rail in the water is photogenic, but the boat was not designed to sail with her rail buried. Her keel was tilted at a forty-degree angle, severely limiting its purchase in the water, so she was sliding and coming toward us like a crab as her helmsman turned her to compensate for the slide. The sails were too taut. A sailboat is pulled forward by the vacuum on the lee side of the sail; her sails were not creating a vacuum. She moved at all only because it is hard to stop a good boat.

I wondered if he ran his company the same way he sailed his boat. Probably.

A friend of mine, a consultant and speaker, claims that corporations use 10 percent of their human potential. He reports that he has said this in the best-managed corporations and gets no argument, just grins and winks of approval. Most companies run with little sense of the wind.

An enormous wind has been blowing since the beginning of humankind. It is that force that insists that we improve as a race, and that each of us add a little to what our parents have given us. The name of the wind is a matter of faith, but the fact that the wind blows is not. Although I cannot see it, I can feel it blasting against my cheeks and whipping the fringes on my parka. The corporate vice president, shortly after getting his new position, wonders what challenge is next. The administrator, pursuing her master's degree, is unsure of where she is going but is sure that she must go there. The factory worker, delighting in learning applied statistics, gains control over the work that used to control him. The father and mother attend parent-effectiveness training. The young man with Down's syndrome accepts the challenge of being a busboy. The woman approaching retirement studies to be a deacon. All of them are answering some call to be more than they presently are.

And what of the corporate helmsman? He tightens the sheets of regulatory systems to the breaking point. He lays the vessel on her side with operational reviews that look good but waste everyone's time. He takes pride in tight budget control—so tight that his subordinates can find no room for their own initiative. He selects his crew based on their apparel and not their competence, and he grins and waves happily, for his corporation succeeds.

A friend of mine, the captain of the Rainbow Connection, let a friend of his take the wheel of his boat. The friend oversteered. First, impatient with the speed of the rudder's response, he would throw the wheel tight to starboard. Then, when the boat began a rapid turn, he would throw it tight to port. Finally, the boat began to sail a straight line. The captain complimented the neophyte helmsman on his newly acquired skill before he realized that the steering cable had been broken. For two miles the boat had been sailing herself as the helmsman proudly spun the wheel from side to side.

Of course the overmanaged corporation succeeds. It is hard to stop a good boat. Given the power of thousands of individual human beings striving to reach their potential, corporate failure is difficult to achieve.

But it makes me sick to see an overcanvased boat dragging her rail. I want to scream back in anger down the harbor, "Ease off! Let her up! She is a good boat, a wonderful vessel. Please let her sail!"

LESSONS FROM THE PLAYGROUND

To UNDERSTAND THE MEN AND WOMEN OF THE CORPORA-tion and their sometimes volatile relationship, I find it helpful to remember that they were not so long ago the boys and girls of the playground.

I never understood the girls' playground and do not claim to understand it now. I have a couple of ideas about it, no more, and so I refer to the boys' playground, the one on the other side of the old church building, which I fig-ured out instinctively early on and of which I have now a decent intellectual grasp.

The first thing I understood about the boys' playground was my role in it. I was not skillful at sports, being slow of foot and not good at raising my voice and showing my muscles to make my point. I learned that when we ran out to play baseball shouting our positions, the primary fight would be who got to bat. I always screamed, "Everlasting first base," and plunked myself on the bag. When the war was over, the vanquished departed to the field, the win-ners were at bat, and I was unchallenged at the position I loved to play anyway.

I was never tempted to play on the girls' playground. First of all, there were girls there, which in my early years meant creatures beneath my consideration and in the junior high years meant creatures capable of turning me to jelly with their budding feminine charms, physical and otherwise.

Second, I could never understand what they did there.

Take jumping rope for instance. How did you win at jumping rope? I am not sure you can, certainly not without the help of two of your foes who are swinging the jump rope. I didn't understand a game without winners and still don't really. My wife refuses to play volleyball with me because I won't let the women on my team spike. I say, "I don't let short people spike, because they will lose the game." She says, "It's no fun to play volleyball if you can't spike." I say, "I played football for twelve years. Because I was slow and wide of frame, I played tackle. I caught one pass in twelve years, and that was because my roommate was quarterback and called a tackle-eligible play three times in a row for my sake." My wife says, "That doesn't sound like fun. You should have quit."

Remember when the teacher would ask a question and all the girls would be squealing with hands in the air, "Sister, Sister, call on me"? (Mine was a parochial school.) If a boy did it, however, we tormented him back on the playground: "Show-off!" "Teacher's pet!" (The word now in my sons' schools is *nerd*.) If he didn't get the message, we ostracized him, pure and simple. We boys were in league against the teacher, as we are against our management now.

My sister would tell me who was mad at whom and who liked whom on her playground, and I was shocked at what they would do to one another in response to some imagined slight. I had one friend like that. He would play the "now we're friends and now we're not" game with me enough to give me a sick feeling in my stomach. That gave me some inkling of what it would be like to live as my sister did, with a coterie of friends constantly examining their relationships and realigning their loyalties, with every move fraught with interpersonal consequence.

I think men and women were raised in completely different worlds. The parents of my son's hockey team got together the other afternoon. For a while the men domi-

nated the conversation, with assertion followed by coun-
terassertion. I said little, although I was tempted to
scream "Everlasting first base." Then the men migrated to
the gym and the women took over. The tone shifted and a
circle gradually was formed, with inquiry followed by
counterinquiry. I said nothing. I couldn't figure out who
was trying to say what, or if anyone was trying to say anything. I know we were raised in different worlds.

"She's not a team player," one hears in the corporation.
That's reasonable; with no teams on the girls' playground,
where would she learn the unconscious reactions that
cover for one teammate's weaknesses and exploit another's
strengths?

"He relies on assertion to get his way." Right: It worked
for him on the playground, and he thinks it's working for
him now.

"He's insensitive to feelings." That was a very helpful
ability on the boys' playground. Try playing football and
being sensitive to feelings.

"She's trying to impress the boss." You better believe it,
and it's working too, isn't it? She still likes to get A's.

Oh, well, the old mores have been fun, but I think they
are changing. Recently I watched a girls' basketball tournament. Mary Jo Miller, Miss Basketball of Minnesota,
not only has a jump shot but she passes, and she uses her
butt to clear out opponents. And she has a teammate who
does nothing on offense but set picks. I think I can hear
the coach: "You're slow of foot and wide of frame and
can't shoot. Your role is to set picks." Take it from an old
pick setter, that girl is a team player, and will be when she
becomes a woman.

The other day, during the sparring session at karate
class, my eleven-year-old son, David, caught an incoming
opponent square in the stomach with a solid side kick.
The other kid, obviously in distress, tried to keep fighting.
David dropped his hands and said, "Let it out. You must

let it out." So his opponent cried for a minute, and then they went back to sparring. Now where did David learn that? Not on my playground, he didn't.

The playground is producing a new breed, which will, in time, create a new dynamic in the relationship between men and women in the corporation. In the meantime I suggest we grant one another the courtesy and forgiveness we would grant someone from another planet. The playground that I was raised on and the playground my sister was raised on separated only by the old church building, were at least a light-year apart.

MUCH ADO ABOUT
A LOOSE PASS

CENTRAL HIGHLAND BEAT HENRY BY ONE GOAL IN OVER-time. The newspaper account credited Pat with scooping up a "loose pass" in the neutral zone and beating the goalie on the glove side for the winning goal. And he deserves the credit. The loose pass and he connected when he had a half-step on one defenseman but had another one to beat on his own. He made a magnificent single-handed rush. Well done!

But I want to talk about that loose pass. It came from our center, who had caught up with an attacker in our zone, squeezed underneath him, hoisted him off the puck, put his own stick on it, and severely hampered by the 175 violent pounds still attached to his back, twisted in an attempt to dump the puck into the neutral zone. Then he spotted Pat cutting across the center of the ice and screwed his own stick around another couple of inches to lay that puck, shimmering with potential glory, three feet in front of Pat, who picked it up and made the paper.

Nor is that all. Thirty seconds before, a competent pair of defensemen had been sent onto the ice to replace our two star defensemen, with the order (I heard it): "Do not forget to play defense." Mindful of those instructions from a coach who resembles a professional football lineman, they did nothing heroic or foolish when Henry attacked. They backed up, and when the Henry center crossed our blue line, he found himself facing two quite competent players, either or both of whom would flatten him if he took one more step. He looked to the left, where his favorite scorer was racing down the boards and could not find him because our back-checking right wing already had him lined up to be removed from the play if he received the puck. It was at that moment of hesitation that he was caught and that loose pass came to be.

My point? Five guys and one coach were responsible for that goal. Why do we give one guy all the credit?

So it is not just in this game but in all games, and at work too. When I was at Honeywell during a severe turn-down, our division executives would not consider cutting the training department. Was it their respect for the genius of people like me, highly trained and presumably skilled technicians of some exotic arts? No. I suspect that if they had known we were there, they would have cut us with pleasure. Whenever they heard the word "training," they thought of the after-hours program. Susan ran that. Her job classification was "clerical." Hundreds of people attended, reported immense learning, and demonstrated practical improvement. My "touchy-feely" job was saved because I was credited with the effects of Susan digging in the corners.

At Control Data, I had the task of judging Ron and informing him that his career had topped out. Ron ran an unsophisticated technical training program. Once a year he had line executives appoint a panel of experts from their organizations to tell him what courses to add to the curriculum, describe the course objectives, and name the teacher. Ron then hired the teacher, told him the objectives, scheduled one running of the course and had it videotaped. He reproduced the handouts, collected them in binders, and distributed them, along with about twenty copies of an invariably grainy videotape, across the country. Engineers viewed these amateurish videotapes with zeal, taking notes all over the handouts. Whenever I met with line executives, I would always slip into the conversation that Ron reported to me. It helped my credibility considerably but not Ron's future. He was not state-of-the-art.

I don't know what the world is thinking when it pays an executive millions for saving a company. (I don't know what it is thinking when it pays an executive millions for ruining a company either, but that is another story.) Not that the successful executive does not deserve something. But what about the other people who dug in under that executive's leadership and did the job? They get to keep their positions, but that's about it. I was reading a Japanese author's book on management in which he spent a page describing the formula invented by an assembly worker, which assembly worker was repeatedly named with great respect. Here, if one of our consulting gurus had written the book, I suspect he would have attributed the formula to himself. Am I harsh?

I do not know just what I want in business terms, but I can say it in hockey. When you score a goal, do not leap up and down in self-congratulation. Go to the guy who passed it to you and thank him, and then go to every other player on the ice and congratulate him. You have room to share your glory; tomorrow you will be in the paper. They will not.

SMALL DECENCIES

My sailboats have never had many instruments. The last two have had a compass. The two before that had not even that. Of course they have all been small boats, starting with a twelve footer, moving to fourteen, then the big leap to twenty-five, and then backing up to twenty-three. If I jammed the wind with a thirty footer, I might buy a wind-direction indicator, a wind-speed indicator, a depth sounder, radar, and Loran-C. I see stuff like that hanging from the masts of the bigger boats, but at my size boat it seems a bit much.

I do have a sort of instrument on which I am extremely dependent. I don't buy it. At the start of every season my wife brings down new ones, garnered from her knitting bag. It consists of two pieces of yarn, about six inches long, the color dependent on what sweater or mittens she was knitting at the end of the winter season. Last year they were red, fading to pink as the season ended. They are tied to the shrouds about five feet off the deck, and there they flutter from spring to summer to fall, usually deteriorating over the winter. They are called telltales.

My eyes seldom leave them when I am at the tiller. Even when I take in the passing sights or calculate my way past other boats, at least out of the corner of my eye I watch the windward telltale to see if its direction shifts, if it moves limply or, most frightening, stiffens and lifts above the horizontal plane. It foretells me of the wind about to strike my sail.

One day I took some friends sailing. It was quiet, with a

warm sun and a niggling breeze. In the midafternoon the breeze freshened, and at last we were sailing with the rushing sounds a sailboat makes as it divides the waters on a perfect day. Relaxed as they were, I am sure my friends were startled at the urgency with which I called for them to bring the sails down, the speed with which I lowered and started the motor, my insistence at tying everything securely. What I had seen was the telltales change from streaming straight to suddenly hanging limply. Thirty seconds after we readied the boat, a fifty-mile-an-hour wind drove us over on our side, with no sails up. God knows what would have happened if the telltale had not signaled the coming trouble.

I am a little claustrophobic. I hate elevators and become quite uncomfortable in small closed spaces. Once when I was visiting a potential client, I had ridden eight floors on the elevator, stopping on every floor, each time fearing that this time the doors would not open. On the eighth floor I emerged, only to find myself locked into a small glass anteroom. She had warned me of this, although no one who is not claustrophobic could have anticipated the terror beginning to rise in me. No need for worry, the phone that she had told me about, which I could use to call her to the door, was there. I lifted the receiver, and before I could dial, a voice answered me. It was someone from the building maintenance department. This phone was for emergency calls to them only.

I did get in eventually. I attracted some attention by rapping on the glass, and a passing employee let me in. After the introductions to my potential client, I wryly told her my story of the funny, if traumatic, thing that had happened on the way to her office. I did not tell it in a tone of recrimination, rather I described my own phobic vulnerability. She was uninterested, neither sympathetic nor apologetic. I don't know if the fact that the phone could not be dialed to contact her even registered. We went immediately to business.

When the telltales point up, look out for a blast of evil wind. In this office, I saw telltales pointing up.

The small decencies we owe one another interest me. Not in themselves, but as telltales of what is to come. I thought about telling this potential client that I could not work for her, making up an excuse, but it was one of those times in my consulting career that I needed work. I listened to her carefully, went away and wrote up what she had told me, and created an approach to meet her needs. She called me on receipt of my proposal and told me that I had missed her point. She invited me back for another try.

I do not usually miss the point. I listen well. When I am rejected as a consultant, usually I am told that I heard the potential client, but he or she just does not like my approach to the problem. Ignoring the telltales, I returned. She described her needs again. They were completely different from the time before. I would test my recollection by reading verbatim from my notes from the first meeting, and she would say that that was not her concern. At the end of this listening session she invited me to try again. This time I paid attention to the yarn. I told her that I doubted that, having failed so badly before, I would hit the target the second time. I took my permanent leave, pleasantly, I hope, and certainly influenced by the fact that once again I had stood tapping at the glass of the confining elevator anteroom.

As I come in the door of a business for the first time, I automatically check the telltales. Is there a place for the visitor's coat? Am I offered a cup of coffee? Am I an interruption to the receptionist or a welcome guest? Am I to wait for my appointment, or does the person who called me in arrive immediately and with enthusiasm at my appearance? Is the phone put on hold? Is there time to talk? A place on the table for my notebook? Adjustments made for my well-being?

These things are inconsequential in themselves. I do not need these as comforts. They are no more important to me in themselves than the idle vagrancies of a few inches of colored yarn. But as an indicator of the spirit of the person I am meeting or the business I am dealing with, these small decencies are excellent telltales. Their absence screams of personal disrespect, harried and overworked people, a harsh or cold atmosphere, an environment corrosive to the human spirit. Their presence almost infallibly suggests caring, time for thought and reflection, and attention to the needs of people beyond the need for a cup of hot coffee.

The other day I made my first call at a company. I had talked to the CEO on the phone and was to meet with him and his personnel vice president. When I came in the door, it was clear that I was expected. The president's assistant immediately answered the receptionist's call, told me he would be late, took my hat and coat, and settled me in a conference room. The personnel man joined me immediately and after the social amenities began asking me some pointed questions about my business and approach. When the president arrived, the personnel man suggested that if the CEO knew all the things he was asking and wished to use the next few minutes for something else, he should go ahead. The president thanked him and said he was willing to listen.

After two hours of exploring the subject, they told me that they would have to think my proposal over. They would call me. I left smiling. I thought I had the contract, although I was not certain. I was positive that I would be fairly treated. In their decency to me and to each other I had seen two pieces of pink yarn streaming steadily in a compassionate breeze.

THE CURMUDGEON

I WAS CHATTING LONG DISTANCE WITH MY FRIEND PAUL the other day when he referred to me as a "loveable curmudgeon."

"A what?" I said. He stuck to his guns. He explained himself some, but basically he would not back up. I did not admit it to Paul, but this phrase has been appearing from other sources, inserting itself into my consciousness. Which annoys me no end.

As I said to Paul, "I am very patient, and very forgiving when you consider how irritating people are." On reflection, I realize that a decent working definition of a loveable curmudgeon is someone who tries to be patient and kind despite the fact he finds people irritating.

But what can I say, except that I do? I do not find everyone irritating, and I do not find anyone irritating all of the time, but there is a lot of human behavior that simply drives me up the wall. I have no idea why people tolerate these things in others, or allow them in themselves.

The following are some examples:

• People not being on time.

Particularly people not being on time for appointments in their own office. Particularly people not being on time for appointments in their own office or their own backyard when I have driven over ten miles to be there on time. In the same class fits people calling at the last minute to say they cannot come, but want to reschedule for a time that they most likely cannot honor either.

• People telling me how busy they are.

My suppressed response is to tell them that most people I know who are accomplishing anything of worth are not terribly busy. I think half of the work that busy people are doing does not need to be done anyway, so I suggest not bragging about it. If you have to be busy, conceal the fact. And do not make it your excuse for not being on time.

• People saying nice things that are not true, even when they say them about me.

Undeserved praise makes me feel as if someone has poured a bottle of syrup on my head. Compliments become meaningless. Criticism becomes gauche, reality foggy.

• People not listening.

In my last six years of consulting to business and government, the only time that I have become openly angry was with a person who did not listen. My frustration at having him screw up a conversation by saying things that directly contradicted everything that had been said before finally released my steam valve. I wouldn't mind his disagreeing, but he treated everybody else's words as if they had not been spoken. Of course, my anger did little good. He didn't hear that either.

• People being patient with people who do not listen.

People who do not listen will only be cured by having other people lose their tempers with them, repeatedly and frequently.

• People seeing with tunnel vision.

There are people who think that the only way to do anything is the way that they already do it, that the only people worth talking with are those carrying their company logo, and that an outside vendor such as myself is out to rip them off. There is a more virulent stage of this disease that limits vision to one's own division and even to one's own department. And there are quite a few genuine basket cases that can see nothing as valuable unless they did it themselves.

• People insisting on stupid meetings.

This too is related to patience. The reason that stupid meetings are allowed to continue is that people who know they are stupid do not say so. If one person would challenge what is going on, five would jump into the fray with glee. The meeting would either be improved or be over. This leads me to one of the most irritating of all phenomena,

• People being patient. Everyone deserves fifteen minutes of tolerance before being told they are off base. Some people deserve thirty minutes of tolerance. It takes them a while to clarify their point. Nobody deserves forty-five minutes of tolerance. For forty-five minutes of tolerance, hire a therapist, don't use me. Patient people do the world the injustice of allowing it to wallow in its errors. Further, patient people frequently go home convinced of their own superiority, when if they had bothered to challenge the evident ignorance of the other person, they may have found that person quite capable of reaching for a deeper truth not seen before.

• People knowing they are right and the other side is wrong.

Life is not a deck of cards with good cards being dealt to my side and bad cards being dealt to the other side. There is no error that lacks truth and no truth that lacks error. I find myself arguing for positions that I do not hold simply because I am so annoyed that the other person feels he or she is incontrovertibly right.

• People getting paid seventy thousand dollars a year plus benefits worth another fifty thousand for doing nothing but getting in the way of people who are trying to do something.

Frequently these are called staff positions. For example, the bean counter who fails to send me a check because the wrong corporate employee signed the invoice and, rather than telling anybody what she is doing, shelves the whole matter, until four months later, someone has the shrewdness to ask her what is going on.

- People calling me when they're in trouble because they've heard that networking is a good idea.

I help people in trouble, but I am a great deal more eager to help someone who called me when I was in trouble, or at least called me when neither of us were in trouble. Some people try to do mechanically what can only be done organically.

- People being unable to experience feeling.

They do things because of what they are feeling but do not know why they are doing them. They do not do things that anyone with an ounce of feeling would do. What irritates me even more is that as a group they feel superior to people with feelings, quite unaware that they are going through life nearly blind and fairly deaf. Frequently they land on their noses precisely because someone whose feelings they have hurt trips them. For a moment this makes me happy. Unfortunately, I am a feeling person, so I end up feeling sorry for them. This is doubly irritating: they mess up my emotional life both when they are up and when they are down.

- People not doing what they said they would do.

This is a compound problem. By the third time I have asked them to do what they said they would do, I get the distinct impression that they are offended at my persistence. Worse, I begin to apologize for reminding them that they have failed me.

- People calling me a loveable curmudgeon.

Can you think of a better way to spike someone's guns? After wearing that label, I might as well stop talking. I can say anything, and the response is, "Isn't he sweet. Such a loveable curmudgeon."

You may have noticed that I have not included on this list "people telling rambling stories only remotely connected to their point." That and a few other things is what I do in an effort to make loveable curmudgeons of my friends.

IN PRAISE OF SLOTH

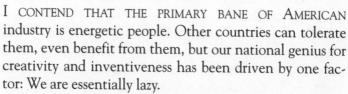

I CONTEND THAT THE PRIMARY BANE OF AMERICAN industry is energetic people. Other countries can tolerate them, even benefit from them, but our national genius for creativity and inventiveness has been driven by one factor: We are essentially lazy.

We invented the automobile because we were too lazy to walk. We invented the steamboat because we were too lazy to paddle. We invented the typewriter to avoid picking up a pen. And we invented the light bulb because we were too lazy to strike a match.

This innate talent, once characteristic of anyone between the Pacific and the Atlantic, north of the Rio Grande, has been nearly totally overcome by a new and foreign-born ethic of industriousness.

When I consulted at a seminar in Washington, D.C., I was impressed by people who would dash for the telephone at the lunch hour, waving their pink slips, "to return their calls." Of course no one was there to receive the calls they were returning. After all, it was lunch hour. But now the other person had a pink slip to prove that the person who returned the call was industrious. And the seminar participant could call his or her own office in a couple of hours and receive another set of pink slips from the same set of people whose secretaries had been contacted over the lunch hour and now were calling back again. The tumult was wonderful. Nothing was accomplished, but at least no one rested.

A friend of mine had a terrible reputation for laziness

among his colleagues. Against opposition, including mine, he pursued a brilliant idea for making money. Money kept pouring in. But he had set his system up so that it ran almost without his intervention. "Well, yeah," we used to say, "he is making more money than anyone else, but he doesn't work hard enough."

I once set up a pilot course for a computer-based training module aimed at executives. I contacted twenty executives to test the course, knowing that only ten of them would respond. Naturally, all twenty wrote me back, expressing enthusiasm for the opportunity and assuring me they had blocked out the time from their busy schedules to be in the computer room at the assigned hour. We had only ten terminals. My partners in this escapade assured me that we could scrounge up the other ten from around town. I thought for a few seconds and changed the design. Ten executives would take the module. The other ten would be buddied with them and record their difficulties with the course. The pilot worked better than the original design would have. My creativity was fueled by my laziness. Not for me, driving around town heaving terminals into my hatchback, lugging them up the steps, crawling on the floor in my three-piece suit, plugging them in, screwing up the wiring, handling the complaints for every bug that develops in them after they are returned. I'd rather think. It's easier.

What would it be like if laziness were widespread? People would do it right the first time, because that is so much easier than fixing it later. People who don't read *The Wall Street Journal* would stop subscribing to it, saving approximately one forest a year. Accounting systems would be simplified by people who ask for only the data they need and consider the simplest manner of collecting it. In baskets would be emptied in three minutes, 80 percent into the circular file. Meetings would stop when they were no longer accomplishing anything. No one would watch the network news. Management structures would be slimmed. Copying machines would be illegal, on the principle that the writer must suffer at least as much as the reader. Everything would be put to the test of usefulness and at least half of the activities of American business would fail the test. With the leftover energy we could cure cancer or the common cold.

This should become a movement: The Return to Laziness. Its clarion call: "Why the blank would I want to do that?" Its motto: "Thought should precede action." Its organizing principle: "Less is better." Its coat of arms: a lion, very passant. The first question on the screening test: "Do you like sixty-hour weeks? " (If you do, find another movement.) Its bible: the *Tao Te Ching*. Its purpose: finding the easier way.

This should become a movement, with articles, brochures and systematization. Seminars too, and books, videos, and tapes to play in the car. But I am too lazy to bring it off. Thank God for that.

THE PARKVIEW CAFE

LAST SUMMER I NEVER CLIMBED THE HILL TO THE PARKVIEW Cafe. Neil, Joe, and Sue had opened a restaurant right in the marina building, and I could go straight from the shower to breakfast done by a professional cook. There was rarely anyone there for breakfast, so this year, minding their costs, they do not open until eleven on weekdays. Now when I am down on the *Hummingbird* by myself, I eat breakfast at the Parkview, supper at the marina, and buy a sandwich at the Cenex store to eat while sailing the boat.

My boat is sailing better than ever before. Since I have an absurdly deep keel, I have had to crank it up ten turns of the winch to adjust for lower water in the marina. This week, for the first time in five years, I forgot to lower the keel ten turns before sailing. I discovered my error when the boat began to sail 50 percent better than before. She points higher and develops less weather helm, because the keel has moved back to the center of effort. This is all very logical, now that I have accidentally done it. There seems to be a lesson in this for those of us who try to control the universe by following the manufacturer's directions.

There is another place to eat in Pepin, the Harborview Cafe, immediately across the railroad tracks from my boat. The Harborview is justly famous for its cuisine. People drive for an hour and a half from the cities and wait outside nearly as long for a table. I seldom eat there.

About a year and a half ago, after a sailing day, I

wanted a whiskey sour and decided to push through the crowd up to the Harborview bar. Five steps inside the door I found myself face to face with another customer. He was about my age, trim of waist, with a twenty-five-dollar silver-gray haircut, immaculate white short shorts, and a white shirt open at the throat. In his left hand he held a martini, and he waved his right hand excitedly as he explained something to three listeners.

Now, you may think him a sailor. I assure you he wasn't. Sailors don't look like him, they look like me. Their hair is in disarray. They are sweaty. Their shorts are filthy dirty. They are dehydrated, exhausted, and in my case, they are overweight.

We stared at each other in mutual shock. He froze only a moment before returning to his conversation, and I stood there only a moment before turning back to the marina. I can clean up my act and wave my martini with the best of them. But I am not going to do it down here. I am eating supper at the marina, and breakfast at the Parkview.

At the Parkview nobody waves their hands with excitement. This has something to do with the number of pickup trucks in the parking lot with the word *Farm* across the top of the license plates. I sit inside the door to the left, as should you if you ever visit there. It is the transient dock; locals turn right and sit either at the counter or squeezed into the big round table.

This morning the waitress, who I think is also the owner, has left work to pick up her daughter, who has hit a deer up by Maiden Rock. In the middle of my breakfast they return. The daughter, about twenty years old, is obviously distraught, and wonders if she should call a cop, since the deer is lying just off the road, next to her disabled car. Her mother points out that the Pepin town cop is in the room and might be able to call one of his buddies, but he declines direct involvement in the case. She considers calling her uncle, who is sheriff, but somebody points out that he is sheriff of Pepin County and Maiden Rock is in the next county. So she decides to call the cop up at the Rock despite the arguments of several that the young guy up there is just part-time and won't be on duty at this time in the morning.

As she heads for the phone, she turns for a moment and says, "The worst thing is that before it died, that deer just stood there and looked at me."

The conversation continues as she makes her call. By the time she returns, the town cop is standing at the cash register, paying his bill. Pretending to concentrate on counting his change, he says to her with mock gravity, "Now, let me get this straight. The deer looked at you, and then it died."

And then, just as she begins to forget her anxiety long enough to comprehend the joke, pocketing his billfold with his left hand, he reaches out with his right arm, pulls her against his side, and gives her the gentlest hug.

I come back from the safe harbor of Pepin to my business life and I sail better for a while. To adjust to the eddies of a small town, I have moved the keel back about ten clicks, but as soon as I sense the blasting winds of the city I am compelled to lower it again, to be configured the way management manuals say I should be configured, goal-oriented, with vision focused, time managed, and results measured.

Could a person survive, or even succeed, with the keel drawn back a little? With time for the caprice of a little meaningless chat? A moment to offer assistance to a fellow struggler? A few seconds for a small joke, a gentle hug? Relief from the constant worry of making the best living possible?

I hope that one of these days I'll pull out of Pepin, forget to turn back the crank, and discover myself sailing more gently, no matter what the wind or waves.

PROGRESS

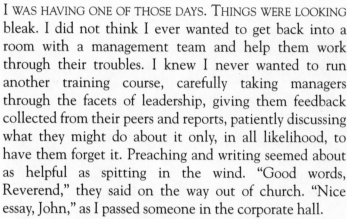

I WAS HAVING ONE OF THOSE DAYS. THINGS WERE LOOKING bleak. I did not think I ever wanted to get back into a room with a management team and help them work through their troubles. I knew I never wanted to run another training course, carefully taking managers through the facets of leadership, giving them feedback collected from their peers and reports, patiently discussing what they might do about it only, in all likelihood, to have them forget it. Preaching and writing seemed about as helpful as spitting in the wind. "Good words, Reverend," they said on the way out of church. "Nice essay, John," as I passed someone in the corporate hall.

"So what," I said this day. It was one of those days when I thought I had not accomplished much with my life except collecting money for room and board.

How much good had my running instrumented labora- tories done for Honeywell and later Control Data? I could point to no remarkable changes. Of the hundred teams I have tried to help, how many were appreciably better? Of the two thousand people I have counseled, how many made a radical and lasting change in their life? Few, or very few, or damn few, it seemed to me.

When my feelings and I are not quite in sync, I like to walk. There is something about walking that sorts out my feelings. So that day I walked with as little purpose as I felt my life had.

Although I did not enjoy the Saint Paul Seminary that much when I attended it, by some coincidence I have spent twenty years of married life geographically close to it. Within half an hour I was pumping along the campus where it borders the Mississippi River. I needed a break. I am not a fast or efficient walker. I have been passed by an old lady with a cane. Just yesterday I was passed by two Oriental men, well under five feet tall. I tried for a while to match their pace. Even when I stepped with their steps, I slowly drifted behind. This seems physically impossible. I have longer legs. But that is the inefficient walking me, and that is why I needed a rest.

I slowed down, lit a pipe. I dropped off the Mississippi Drive sidewalk, under the old stone bridge, to the path that leads up the ravine into the seminary grounds. I went to the grotto of the Blessed Virgin Mary. The statue of Mary had been removed and the whole area looked untended. Apparently Marian devotion had hit upon hard times in the Roman Catholic church. But the walls were still there.

The walls were created in '58, '59, and '60. One steep side of the ravine tended to slide into the creek every spring. The strategy concocted before my time was to build a set of three rock dry walls, one above the other, and remove the dirt in between them so that instead of one steep incline there would be three level platforms. It was easier said than done.

I don't know what led me to join the crew in '58. But I did. A dry wall at its surface looks like single rows of rock piled one on another, at a severe slant. That is not what it is. To create a dry wall five feet tall, we first dug back about five feet into the bank until we had created a five-foot horizontal floor and a perfectly vertical five-foot bank; the completed wall was about thirty feet long. To do this we had to remove 325 cubic feet of clay and dirt by shoveling it into wheelbarrows and pushing the wheelbarrows across a small bridge and up a fifty-foot trail to be dumped over an embankment another forty feet closer to the river. When we finished removing the dirt, a truck deposited large loads of rock at the end of the trail, and we loaded the wheelbarrows, rolled them down to the bottom of the ravine and over the bridge, then lifted them into the hole where the dirt had been, assembling them first in a five-foot-deep jigsaw puzzle, and then ever smaller puzzles until we had created 325 cubic feet of rock retaining the hill at that level.

This process we repeated three years in a row. Now, thirty-one years later, I am looking at the results. They are a little weathered, but I must say they look better for it. "Now, there is one thing you accomplished in your life that nobody can deny," I said to myself. This did not cure my depression. Three abandoned rock walls do not a satisfying career make.

But they did give me a key, for as I looked at them, I realized that I did not build them. We built them. There were about twenty young men who every week devoted several hours of their precious free time to digging and hauling. I was more consistent than some and more sporadic than others. But I was one among many. We built it.

I walked across the bridge onto the first plateau, leaned against the wall of '59, and began to rethink my career not from the perspective of what I had done, but from the perspective of what we had done.

In 1969 when I, a product of the church and the human relations training movement, entered the Honeywell Ordinance Division eager to change the world of business into a better place for humans to be, everyone was male, wore a crew cut, and was addicted to sitting in rows and being told what to do.

This is an exaggeration, but an exaggeration based on truth. Not too long ago I reviewed an industrial movie of that era presenting some famous speaker or other talking to a business audience. Everyone in that audience, which the camera panned from time to time, was exactly as I have described him, with the addition of a blue suit, a white shirt, and a narrow, dark-colored tie. There was one woman in the group of about fifty; she wore a dark blue skirt, a dark blue jacket, a white blouse, and a dark blue bow at the neck. She did not have a crew cut.

At my instrumented laboratories I would frighten the guys (in two years there was only one woman, two Orientals, one black), by giving them round tables to sit at and refusing to appoint a group leader. When they appeared comfortable with that situation, I would remove the tables altogether, provoking terror anew.

When I took a team off-site, everyone would seek my personal reassurance that this was not sensitivity training and that nobody would crack up in the course of the meeting. Almost everyone concealed their feelings in an attempt to appear perfectly rational in everything they did.

Of the participants at training events that I now conduct, close to half are female, with a broader representation of people of color. They tend to come from diverse backgrounds, with diverse attitudes, diverse training, diverse personal objectives, and a greatly enhanced desire that they be taken seriously and not be expected to give up their personal style to a monolithic corporate methodology.

The reaction to feeling words is radically different. Many have been in therapy or counseling for family problems. Many are members of twelve-step organizations. Most have read self-help books in the field of psychology. Not only are they not afraid of "sensitivity training," frequently their concern is that I have not led them deeply enough in the exploration of the group psyche.

Indeed, where I once could rely on ignorant dependence in my clients, now I am likely to be challenged. "When Brice did this, he did it differently." "Jeri would not stick her oar in as often as you do." Line managers have now experienced being human at work for themselves, and they are quite prepared to challenge me when I am not human enough for them.

While I still do not see in people the radical personal-growth changes I had once hoped I would, I now see them quick to listen to one another and understand one another's style, and shrewd enough to grasp the value of adaptation to it. They want to know where the other person's buttons are, so that they can push the ones that will produce the desired effects.

Where once I had hoped for a type of humanization in which people would put people first and the job second, I am now quite pleased with the results of a healthy inter-action between people and work. Once I had hoped to turn work into a human relations group. Now I realize that people are formed, and formed better, when they create, although they look quite different doing that than when the task is simply to sit around and share feelings.

None of this have I done by myself. This movement has evolved over twenty-five years for me and even longer for others. The cause of being human at work has been advanced by twelve-step group organizers, marriage counselors, therapists, self-help authors, preachers, high-school teachers, and other people in the field of organization development.

Nor have our clients been passive recipients of our ministrations. Line managers in their various life roles of husband and wife, parishioner, patient, and alcoholic have sought assistance and growth from those of us both in and out of industry. It has been the line manager who decides to change and grow and make the organization a more human place.

I have been but a drop in the stream. But as a drop, I have made a difference. An hour ago somebody called me to say that he read an essay of mine called "Mother's Day" and decided to see his own mother and tell her he loved her. I did not cause this action. This man has spent the last five years attending lengthy sessions on Gestalt therapy. He is a good man, deeply committed to his own growth. I was only a drop in the stream, but I am pleased to have been that.

I offer this essay to salute all of us who are drops in the stream. My cause has been the humanization of work. Yours might be some other technology or task. Together we can take immense pride in the last twenty-five years. We have done much. We can offer hope to those beginning careers in the work force. Most should be warned that only the exceptional few can point to their own dramatic effect on history. But we, the unexceptional many, can take much credit for what we have done to push the stream along.

I do not know if this is a point of sadness or not. The walls I shared in building—not only the walls of the seminary grotto, but the walls of the personal-growth groups I used to facilitate—now protect an empty shrine. I think there is still something to be gained by revisiting them. In those days and in those groups, I experienced a level of interpersonal peace, a depth of sharing and an underlying trust that has as yet not been duplicated for me or by me in industry.

We still have a way to go. I have ten more years in the work force, perhaps I can nudge it further. And then there is work for the next generation.

I pushed off the wall, brushed the worst of the dirt from my pants, stepped off the plateau, crossed the bridge, and climbed the path. My breath was coming a little quickly. "My," I thought, "I doubt that I could push many full wheelbarrows up that path anymore." Yes, there is work for the next generation.

TEARS

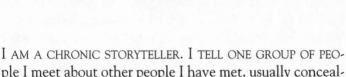

I AM A CHRONIC STORYTELLER. I TELL ONE GROUP OF PEO-
ple I meet about other people I have met, usually conceal-
ing the names of the characters. A new problem is forming for me as a mature businessman who tells stories.
Often when I describe people, I feel the need to cry.

I cannot tell you what it is that I see that moves me so
dramatically. A friend of mine, the former rector of our
church, once wept his way through a description of his
mother for a Mother's Day sermon. As near as I could figure, it was that she left cookies out for him when he came
home from school that so choked him up. He would get to
the word "cookies" and then become incoherent. To this
day I have no idea why the remembrance of cookies after
school would make anyone cry. My mother did the same
for me from time to time, and the remembrance of that
moves me not one whit.

I do not say this to laugh at my old rector, unless it is to
laugh at myself also. When I came home late at night, my
mother always was awake, and would stay awake in case
there was anything I wanted to tell her about my evening.
If I had nothing to say, she never asked. If I had something
to say, she would listen forever. Telling you that makes my
chin tremble. I don't suppose you would know why?

But I bet, as long as we are on mother stories, that you
have one about your mother that arouses equally passionate emotions, the reasons for which you cannot commu-
nicate. I would like for you to have stories similar to these.
Everyone deserves them.

The problem of tears is not new to me. I possess a report card from kindergarten that says that I was emotionally immature. When, in my mature years, I read that, I had to ask my mother what the teacher could have meant. When you are five years old, it's hard to be emotionally immature. The kindergarten maturity standards have to be low. What could I have been like to fail so minor a hurdle? My mother said the teacher meant that I cried a lot for little apparent reason. And now, five decades later, it is happening again.

When I was in junior high at Saint Bridget's on Minneapolis's north side, the pastor was seventy-five-year-old Jimmie Donahue, from Prince Edward Island. Jimmie was a tough nut. Look up Prince Edward Island on a map and you will know how he got that way. It is an unlikely interruption of the North Atlantic, barely classifying as dry ground. Every spring he would start the young people's hiking club. The club would hold one meeting, during which Jimmie would hike the young people's legs off, and after which nobody would come to the next meeting. Which delighted Jimmie, because it proved his basic point: that they were a bunch of softies and he was one tough nut.

I remember the day he gathered a bunch of us boys and informed us that any real man would cry at *Lassie Come Home*. He had seen it eight times and had cried every time. He then tried to describe for us the touching parts but couldn't, because he would start crying, dissolving into inarticulate sobs. He was lord over not only our school and our church but also our homes and our neighborhood. When I was eleven, my local version of the Lord high God declared tears to be virtuous.

But hardly anyone else did. Jimmie was about the only one who said that tears were all right. So I have pretty much succeeded in suppressing them in public, struggling to meet kindergarten standards. In private, my wife finds tears charming on me, and my sons find them embarrassing. "Geez," they say, as they catch me weeping in front of the TV, "are you doing that again?" "But," I say, "Mike Schmidt is retiring. Do you know how good he was? Do you know he became one of the greatest players in baseball with desire and two bad knees?" I had had the same trouble some years ago trying to explain to my oldest son, who was an infant at the time, what it meant that Dorothy Hamill was now "the best."

What moves me is not what you might think. For instance, death bothers me only a little. Since I am long gone from the parish ministry, I am not often called in to death scenes anymore. But the last time I was, as a substitute for the rector who was out of town, I remember once again being the clinical Cowan, dispassionately sorting out what needed to be done, not much impacted by the fact that Chuck's life had suddenly ended and his body lay there, because tough nut that I am, I know well that it will happen to everyone, including me, so why cry about it?

But ask me to describe what manner of man this Chuck was, and the tears begin to well in my eyes. It is as if there are not enough words or gestures to express the strength of my feeling for this man and who he was, even though we were not close. We hardly knew each other. But I had had a glimpse of the kindly furnace that was his heart.

Today in a restaurant I saw a woman with brown hair falling straight to square shoulders, a slender gold necklace tight to her neck, a simple tan blouse, a face plain and unadorned. She did not smile for the waiter, and I wanted to come and ask her how she dared to live in such majesty. I was touched by her simple glory.

People do not have to be dead to merit my tears. Most of those who do are alive. I think the common denominator is that I am moved by who people are, their toughness, their bravery, their tenderness, their loyalty, their fears. I see them all around me as I go about making my living and living my life, and I, occupied with the task of self-survival, barely notice what I am seeing until the moment I try to tell someone else about these people. My memory presents to me a scene that captures a piece of their essence. Then I realize I have no words that offer fitting tribute to who they are, and my feelings find a worthy sacrament only in my tears.

INTEGRITY

DURING THE MONTH OF NOVEMBER FORTY PEOPLE MET AT my house in seven groups ranging from three to ten people. We met to discuss "Belief and Practice," an essay I had written in October. The conversation took many turns. Since most of the people present were strangers to one another, close to half of the time was spent simply meeting. After that, the basic question was, "What interested you about the topic?" and we ranged out from there.

A definite theme was: *How can I be who I am in a world that does not reward me for being me, but rewards me for being someone else?* Person after person reported the stress they experienced in trying to be true to themselves, yet remain a well-paid member of their corporation.

Later that month, on the evening my wife's five-day sickness took a turn for the better, I was sitting with a glass of white wine before a fire, my children occupied in various places, when my Aunt Vickie called. Vickie seldom calls. I am too young to really count in her life picture. It isn't that she doesn't care for me, but she cares as an adult cares for a precocious child. Those old enough to really interest her are mostly dead. Since my mother died and my sisters live in Santa Fe, Vickie now calls me on occasion.

Entranced by the patterns of her voice, I paid only a little attention to what she said, this wife of my long-departed uncle, who played the violin, trained by his own heart and ear, and created close-fitting cabinets. "In the White House, John—you visit there, you should look—it

will say on the inside of the cabinet, 'By David Green.'"
He was the age I am now when cancer took him, and his
eighty-two-year-old wife now sings to me on the phone in
the lilts and slurs of the Swedish accent they all acquired
in Milaca, Minnesota—Vickie and David, Signur, Vivian,
Ruth (my mother), Agnes, and Judith, and their parents,
Emil and Amanda.

She had probably called to tell me that Signur, age
eighty-seven, was in the hospital, but it is not wise to
guess why anyone in my family has called. She mentioned
Sig second, so that was probably the important thing, for
the important thing frequently comes second. If it is very
important indeed, it comes last, squeezed in before end-
ing. She probably did not know for sure why she called
either; perhaps to warn me that she, a last link of my heritage, must die soon also. And then, except for my sisters,
I will be quite alone in these memories.

But her song—for song it is, that accent lilting and
slurring—brings to mind the family gathered. "Look at
John," the men say, "a big strong boy." "Oh, he grows so
big," say my aunts. Chorus and descant blending, year
after year. Ernie, the great-uncle, stands on a chair with
his guitar, compelling song and laughter. Anna, his wife,
feigning embarrassment at his antics—Anna, who cannot
say "good morning" without using five tones of the major
scale. Emil, the grandfather, at five foot five, looms over
the gathering, his carpenter arms bulging through his
dress shirt, his barrel chest threatening the vest buttons.
Grandmother Amanda, guardian of the stove, will eat
there after she feeds the others, steel in the background,
final arbiter of good and evil. The men will sneak a drink
in the basement to avoid her Baptist eyes. My father is
silent at these gatherings, his Irish rapier a little too
deadly and fragile to draw among cheerful Swedish
broadswords. And finally my mother, who dared to marry
the Catholic Irishman against disapproval—loved, feared,

and marveled at by those who created her. "You must ask Ruth," they say to one another. "She will know what to do."

I know that over the years I have gained a reputation for integrity. My friends expect me to take the risk of saying what I see, doing what I must, being who I am. I have my flaws, but this is seen as my strength. Let me now tell you my secret.

When the question is asked, the situation developed, the powerful awaiting my answer, I see a ghostly party pause, my family waiting expectantly in silence. And, whenever I have said what I must say or done what I must do, whatever the response in the room, I hear an invisible chorus and descant: "What a big boy he is!" "Just like his mother!" "His father might have said that!"

It is not that I am not influenced by the opinions of others, but I fear and respect my family chorus more than anyone else I have ever met. And that's how I stay who I am.

Which leads me to two things: First, I plan to take my sons to visit those remaining—Vickie, Signur, Anna, and Ernie—so that when I tell them of those who sang when they spoke, they will know the sound. They will have heard the lilt and slur of the Milaca Swedish accent. Second, for you struggling to be yourself in a world which may or may not reward it, I will pray that one of these evenings when you are quiet and receptive, perhaps with a glass of wine in your hand and a fire before you, *your* Aunt Vickie calls, and if she doesn't, that you have the sense to call her.

SAILING THROUGH
A CAREER

SEVERAL RECENT TASKS HAVE BROUGHT ME TO READ SOME career literature, review some career courses, and talk to some career counselors. My realization being that it's all designed for powerboaters. And I'm a sailor.

For about five years, sailing has been my passion. I now own a twenty-five-foot sloop, docked at Superior, Wisconsin. She is called the *Hummingbird* for her habit of humming to herself at any speed over three knots. I always refer to her as a little boat, because Superior is one heck of a big lake, and most sailors there are piloting boats between thirty and thirty-six feet long. Superior is not a kind lake, but it attracts me with the grandeur of its wickedness.

I have friends on the docks who run powerboats. My favorite person among them is Steve, a charter fisherman. He owns *Hard Times*, a twenty-five-foot inboard-outboard with a flying bridge and more money invested in accessories than I have invested in my entire boat. Steve and I run to help each other land and generally enjoy each other, although we speak quite different languages. Mine is halyards, sheets, and lines, and his is pitch, rpm's, and electronics.

When Steve roars out of the harbor on one of his fishing excursions, he knows precisely where he wants to go and he knows the most direct route. If the fish aren't biting there, he has a backup plan for where to try next. Enjoyment of the journey is not the point at all. I have watched him and his passengers huddled behind shields and bulkheads, *Hard Times* snorting and bucking like a crazed horse eager to dislodge them, banging through the chop. They are intent on getting there. They endure the process.

If the lake is friendly, they troll placidly, focused on their lines, drinking their beers. The marine radio chatters with their conversations as they check out positions and talk to other fishing boats. If the lake is moving, they wobble and roll until their stomachs can take it no longer. If the lake is stormy, they run like heck at twenty-five knots. For all her power, *Hard Times* is an uncontrollable maverick in a crosswind, only reluctantly responsive to Steve's considerable skill. The moment of pleasure comes when they step off onto the dock with the announcement that they have "eleven in the box"—eleven fish to show at home.

Now, sailing is not like that. To start with, I get up when I wake up, not at the ungodly hour Steve and his customers arrive. Actually, there are two wake-ups. The first one is when Steve kicks *Hard Times* over at 5:30 and his engine vibrations disturb my rest. The second is when I can no longer ignore the sun. I eat my breakfast slowly and listen to the weather forecast to plan my day. If Mother Superior is vicious, I am staying in the harbor. If the wind's from the west or northwest, I'm going up the North Shore. If the lake is reasonable, I'll circle Park Point.

None of my voyages are straight lines. To get anywhere with sail involves diagonal courses, each course a compromise between the desired goal and the reality of the wind. But, summed up, I do get there.

My passengers aren't passengers. They are crew. They undo the lines, lift the sails, take their turn on the tiller. The *Hummingbird* provides little shelter. Her cabin is claustrophobic, leading to seasickness on even gentle days. We don't talk much to one another, let alone to other sailboats. Our focus is on the lake. When it's rough, we pay attention to the sailor's cardinal rule: Keep the mast up and the keel down. When it's gentle, our focus is on getting everything from the wind to allow the *Hummingbird* to hum.

She is safe in almost any weather when properly adjusted and only becomes troublesome on the occasions when I must use the motor. She never outruns storms, because she can't. Six knots is all she can do, no matter what. When we return from wherever we've been, we have nothing to show for it but the pleasure of the passage and the one more thing the lake has taught us about ourselves and our boat.

As I say, most of the career literature was written for Steve and *Hard Times*. Unfortunately, the *Hummingbird* and I are sailors.

Although I have a general direction, I don't know for sure what I want to do next. I'm waiting with sails up for the wind to tell me. All I require is that it be worth doing, that it stretch my skills, that I can do it, and that I learn something new while I'm doing it. There are only two things that I won't take—a lake so small that the *Hummingbird* is considered a big boat, and winds so light that I have to use my noisy, foolish motor. I watch my brothers and sisters in industry power by me, tossing me in their wakes, rattling my shrouds and halyards, shaking my mast. And I feel sadness that I am so inadequately left. But then the wind comes. I begin to heel. The sheets are adjusted. The tiller set. The *Hummingbird* hums and I care less where others are gone or going. I hope only that they enjoy their passage as I enjoy mine.

I have no fears that the powerboaters aren't having fun. Both on the lake and in the office they appear happy as they display their catches—the vice presidency, the raise, the special award. Frequently they seem happier than I am, caught in these doldrums, pressured by that gale, or even worse, doubtful about the course.

No, the career literature was designed for them, and I am confident that they will happily churn forward. My fears are for the sailors who don't know they are sailors. I believe I hear them motoring through organizations, their engines badly overworked, their sails under covers and in bags. I see them grimly determined to imitate powerboats. My fear is they will never experience the silent power and freedom of a sail in the wind.

MASTER OF SYSTEMS

SOMETIME AROUND THE FIRST CENTURY A.D., A JEWISH rabbi listed the issues on which a person will be judged when he or she faces God. The last of the seven issues was, "Did you learn how one thing follows another?"

There is a Japanese story of the master of swordsmanship who was introduced to the tea ceremony by a tea master. After the elaborate ceremony of meeting the guest, preparing the tea, serving the tea, drinking the tea, and removing the dishes, the swordsman remarked that at no time during the ceremony had the tea master left himself vulnerable to attack. The discipline of the sword and the discipline of creating tea, when mastered, had led to similar behavior.

I (and quite a few others) posit the existence of an underlying system to life which can be discerned by scientific analysis and described using a language called General Systems Theory. Describing General Systems Theory is not my purpose here. Understanding and behaving in accordance with the underlying system is.

Rabbis have always been extremely practical. The centuries-old advice to understand how one thing flows from another was presented as a practical road to living a happy life as an individual and contributing to the happiness of the community as a whole. Behavior based on understanding of the underlying system will be effective and not frustrating. The person so behaving will not expect what the system cannot give, but will attain that which can be attained, that which benefits one as a part of the system and will benefit the system itself.

System-sensitive people find work relatively easy. They create much with little effort, since they do not do for the system what it will do for itself and they do not push the system to go in directions counter to its basic flow. They are extremely active in bending, forming, and shaping, and avoid saying "but." They believe the first step in a successful business is knowing how the world works.

If this sounds like common sense to you, let me point out that much of what I see and hear is based on a quite contradictory theory: "If everyone goes for what he wants, it will all work out all right for everyone." I once proposed to the chief executive of a major corporation that the corporation hold the following as a value: "The good of the whole corporation shall be considered ahead of the good of any department by the department's executive management." He said that it was unfair to ask for that commitment. To me it seems absurd not to.

How can those of us who do believe in the underlying system find it and come to a practical, working knowledge of it? Following are four pieces of advice.

1. Master at least one system.

Be it chess, market forces, basket weaving, or engineering—know one system in its depth. Go beyond the rules of thumb until you can express in your own words its ins and outs. Go to the point where you seldom find a book or article that tells you anything new about your chosen field. Go to the point where you can accurately surmise that which you have not been told.

The wife of a friend of mine once recommended that he not hire a particular man who was unfaithful in marriage. She never did articulate why that was a reasonable stance. Under our questioning she appeared both moralistic and foolish. Within the week, the potential hire proved unfaithful in business. I learned to respect her as a master of human systems.

2. Learn something else—perhaps two or three things— nearly as well.

To see a flower entirely, it must be seen from several angles, not just one. To understand the underlying system, a person must have an understanding of more than one system. With that comes the capacity to winnow out what was peculiar to the one system and retain that which is common to all.

3. Do not analyze, but experience.

The underlying system is not easily categorized or talked about. It is experienced. The master feels its pulls and tugs.

A friend of mine, a programmer, was found correcting a blueprint of the local golf club's irrigation system. When I asked what a programmer knows about plumbing, he answered, "It feels the same." I had found a master of systems.

4. Measure your gains by the number of your questions, not the number of your answers.

The more you understand, the more answers you will have, but also the more questions. Saints feel like sinners. Wise people feel ignorant. It is what happens when a window opens into the universe. Certainty comes only for those who close the blinds and draw the drapes. The Reverend Ed Gleason, my high-school algebra teacher, was an expert on birds. Show him any bird and he would tell you what it probably was, but he refused to identify even a robin for sure. You will know you are achieving mastery when your early certainties have become fuzzier and you like it that way.

This jotting is in its own way a small test of your mastery of systems. Your willingness to read it at all indicates your ability to look beyond the immediate.

If you followed as I leaped from one system to another—leaped from analogy to abstraction to concrete example—you are potentially a master.

If you understood why the system-sensitive person avoids saying "but," you are already a master of systems.

READING BETWEEN
THE LINES

Once at a workshop panel on organization develop-ment, I and the other panelists were asked how we got into the trade. Dick Byrd startled us all by going back to his childhood to describe his first organization develop-ment experience. His story started me thinking about my childhood as my training ground in this profession.

I come from a dysfunctional family. I am pretty sure of that. I am not embarrassed. There is quite a crowd of us dysfunctionals. If there were a tug-of-war, and in a sense there is, we seem to outnumber the functionals. My fam-ily's first and most glaring dysfunction was the quarrel going on between my parents. While it is sad that an eight-year-old child had the job of peacemaker between two warring adults, it was excellent training for the team-development sessions that were to come later. All other conflicts, in comparison, have been easy to resolve—and much less upsetting to my stomach.

The second dysfunction was that we never spoke of love. Now, I know that in the books this is really bad, and I try to make sure that I speak to my sons of my love. I even tell my wife that I love her, more often than I am inclined to and less often than she deserves. But in my dysfunctional family of origin it was very clear to me that I was loved. Our seldom-spoken family rule was to never say it, just show it by what you do.

While attending the third session of a management-training class in psychocybernetic principles, I asked my fellow participants, "How many have tried to apply these principles?" A scraggly few raised their hands. Another manager asked if I would be interested in how many *planned* to use the principles. Before I could catch myself, I heard my voice, dripping with the contempt I usually veil, say, "Why would I be interested in that?"

In my family you didn't say it, you did it. My father was the paragon of this. My mother did even more than my father, but on occasion she would say something affectionate, thus breaking the rule. When I was fourteen, at the close of the twice-a-month visiting day at the seminary I attended, my father, unable to borrow Grampa's car, arrived in triumph with my tin laundry case, having taken the streetcar from north Minneapolis to downtown, transferred first to Saint Paul, then to north Snelling Avenue, and walked the last four miles. He said, "Here's your laundry." I said, "Thank you."

Or when I was thirty-five and waiting for Edith to give birth to Benjamin. At ten in the evening on the phone to my mother, I complained about walking around in sweaty socks. At midnight my father arrived, having driven from south Minneapolis to my house in Saint Paul and back to Minneapolis. As I recall the conversation, he said, "Here's your socks." And I said, "Thank you."

My family background has been handy training for reading between the lines in the business world, where sometimes words are designed to conceal feelings and intentions. A simple example is hearing from a secretary that someone I have come to see is running late and asks that I make myself comfortable in the waiting room, with no realization that I have traveled across town and come on time and this person cannot make it twenty feet to see me on time. Now tell me I am valued. I feel my eyes doing the same trick my mother's used to, turning down and away. It is not from hurt. It is from embarrassment at having caught the other person in a grievous lie. It is my attempt to conceal that I know what has been said, a pretense at ignoring the passage of wind.

I agree with the psychologists. It is better to speak of love. Remember again my father and that tin laundry box: If he had mailed it the same day he had planned the trip, it would have arrived barely twenty-four hours later than it did. He didn't want to deliver laundry. He wanted to see his fourteen-year-old son.

Love is sometimes more poignant when it is discovered between the lines.

COLORS AND SHADOWS

I WAKE UP AT 6:30 ON THE HUMMINGBIRD. WHEN I CAME down to Pepin, Wisconsin, from the cities yesterday, a twenty-five-knot wind was blowing the length of the lake. This morning it is quiet. I extract myself from the bunk, pull on my sweat suit, and survey the morning. A light mist lifts off the still water.

I have wanted to indulge myself with a giant pancake at the Parkview Cafe ever since I saw one defeat my son on the Fourth of July. I meander down the dock. It's a long dock. I am the twenty-seventh boat from shore. As I almost reach land, a dozen startled ducks explode from between the slips.

I climb fifteen feet up the ramp to the top of the seawall. I turn toward the marina. On my right sits *Tiffany*, a forty-foot motor launch. Last night her children were playing with her dinghy and various floating toys. Now she is blanketed in canvas, sealed until next weekend. To my left, seven miles across the lake to the west, Lake City reflects the glory of the morning sun.

The windows of my car are covered with dew. I start the motor, roll the side windows down and then up, run the wipers and chug up the hill to the Parkview Cafe. Three cars and five pickups fill the tiny space allotted for parking. I enter the cafe. Eight men at a large table turn toward me and stare at this newcomer to their Monday-morning scene. I seat myself on the other side of the cafe. They are now prepared to ignore me, and I, from my corner, can watch old friends waking up together over the morning coffee.

I order the famous pancake. A young man is kidded by the waitress about being late for work. He is not worried. She is an attractive woman in baggy blue jeans and a floppy checkered shirt, both mother and daughter to the cronies' table.

The town cop arrives. They ask him if he succeeded in keeping order over the weekend. They all laugh, for Pepin is too small to need order. They tell him his shirt is growing to match his beef. They laugh again and he sits to join them—a man with a beer belly and massive forearms, taking his rightful place.

The pancake is not what I wanted. I don't finish it. I pay the bill. Pancake plus sausage, plus orange juice, plus coffee equals $2.45. The car rolls back to the marina. I retrace my steps. A muskrat dashes down the south seawall and dives under the dock, intent on avoiding my attention. I climb aboard the *Hummingbird*, light my ceremonial cigar, and begin to write this jotting.

Three freight trains pass, a few minutes apart, their whistles demanding a clear crossing. The town truck—army surplus, 1975—is briefly visible at the top of the hill on Main Street. Two fishermen are now shouting instructions to each other as they prepare their boat, a dirty green johnboat with a huge Evinrude. The flag above the marina begins to signal a lifting breeze.

I came here this day to understand what comes next in this full life I have led for fifty years. I thought it time for some vision for my future, worthy of being passed along. Instead I have seen:

A light mist lifting off still water.
A dozen startled ducks exploding.
A city reflecting the glory of the morning sun.
Old friends waking up together over morning coffee.

A mother/daughter in baggy blue jeans and floppy checkered shirt.

A man with a beer belly and massive forearms taking his rightful place at the table.

A muskrat splashing its way to cover.

A flag, signaling a lifting breeze.

And there, after all, is my message to myself: Do not allow the daily demands to interfere with seeing the colors of the day or the shadows of the night.

The cigar is out, the wind is now definite. It is time to put on the floppy hat my wife bought me—canvas, with the never-blow-off strings. The early morning is over. It is time to sail.

But first, let me see what the ducks are furiously protesting.

ON PLAYING THE FLUTE

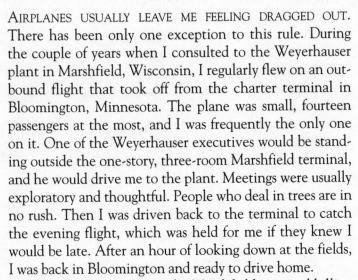

AIRPLANES USUALLY LEAVE ME FEELING DRAGGED OUT. There has been only one exception to this rule. During the couple of years when I consulted to the Weyerhauser plant in Marshfield, Wisconsin, I regularly flew on an outbound flight that took off from the charter terminal in Bloomington, Minnesota. The plane was small, fourteen passengers at the most, and I was frequently the only one on it. One of the Weyerhauser executives would be standing outside the one-story, three-room Marshfield terminal, and he would drive me to the plant. Meetings were usually exploratory and thoughtful. People who deal in trees are in no rush. Then I was driven back to the terminal to catch the evening flight, which was held for me if they knew I would be late. After an hour of looking down at the fields, I was back in Bloomington and ready to drive home.

One day I was sitting in the Marshfield terminal killing time by watching a Cessna "shooting touch and go's." A woman with a girl who looked about seven years old and a boy about five sat across from me, their backs to the runway. We were the only people in the room. Gradually the two children shifted from their prim, seated positions, turning to kneel on the battered, bolted-down folding seats so they too could see the fascinating scene outside. Without looking at them their mother said, "Sit straight." And they did.

I hate that woman to this day. I still grieve for her children.

When my son David was in third grade, my wife was

called in for a conference on his poor behavior. That startled us. We had only been to regular conferences before, and they were always begun with the teacher giggling over David, filled with anecdotes about what he had done or said. They seemed a little in love with him.

But this teacher was different. She was genuinely worried about his waterbug mind. My wife suggested that I not be brought into the discussion since she knew I was the genetic source of his behavior. Instead, the school social worker was sent to investigate David. His report follows:

> I entered unobtrusively from the back of the room. David was the only child who turned to look at me; everybody else was standing and facing the front. The teacher reprimanded him for looking at me. The teacher told them to sit. David's books fell on the floor. The teacher reprimanded him for dropping his books. As he picked them up, the teacher gave directions for the next exercise. He missed the directions. He asked the girl next to him for the directions. The teacher reprimanded him for talking. Not having the directions, he did the exercise incorrectly. She reprimanded him for that.

Having been given the report, I asked David how he survived this teacher. "Aw, Dad, she can't help it. She is just dumb."

I corrected him. "She's not dumb. She just has a marching-band mind. It only works straight ahead."

Many years ago a friend of mine said that the school system prepared people to work in industry. "You mean by teaching basic skills?" I asked.

"No," he said. "It teaches them to sit at a desk, mind their own business, and shut up."

The school my sons attended was normally an exception to this. After a stressful third grade, David again became his teacher's delight.

The school system I went through was twenty-one years of David's third-grade experience. When I began the study of philosophy, a metaphysics professor asked my class, "What will it mean to study philosophy?"

I rushed to answer, "It will mean searching for the meaning of my own life through studying the wisdom of the philosophers." He found that more than a little amusing. His answer was that we would learn every thought that Aristotle ever had.

I have nothing against marching-band minds. I am quite capable of doing a little marching of my own when the situation calls for marching. Drums create a happy ache in my heart. "Pound the drums, gang!" I say, "I will fall into step readily and proudly march with you down the field. But when I begin to improvise on my flute, don't try to shut me up. A person does not live by drums alone."

A new friend of mine, the poetess and spiritual director, Sarah Maney, has a book of poems entitled *Coloring Outside of the Lines*. In industry today, as the clear lines about the right way to conduct business begin to fade, what will we do with a management population that has been trained from the Marshfield airport, to third grade, to Aristotle, through their career to color inside the lines? Be creative, is the call, pound the drum differently, but keep your hands off of that silly flute, sit at your desk and be quiet, wear the same suit as everyone else, read one book, express yourself in the same language as your peers, don't be interested in oddities, and, whatever you do, don't look out the airport window.

I think some critical answers to present problems can be found out the window. More than one philosophy may be useful. Different thoughts require different language. The lilting trill of the flute fits many occasions better than the thump of the drums.

I was in a shopping mall in Toledo when a small Mexican band began to play. Two hundred other people and myself followed them all around the mall, pulled by the free, wild emotion of their songs. Strange that we followed. They didn't even have a drum, just three guitars, one trumpet, one slide trombone, the human voice, and, oh, yes, one silly little flute.

DANCING

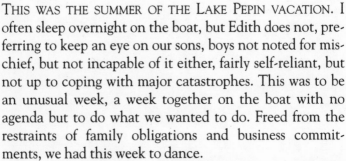

THIS WAS THE SUMMER OF THE LAKE PEPIN VACATION. I often sleep overnight on the boat, but Edith does not, preferring to keep an eye on our sons, boys not noted for mischief, but not incapable of it either, fairly self-reliant, but not up to coping with major catastrophes. This was to be an unusual week, a week together on the boat with no agenda but to do what we wanted to do. Freed from the restraints of family obligations and business commitments, we had this week to dance.

Sometime during the week we heard from Joe, the marina owner, that he was sponsoring a team in the slow-pitch softball tournament. He and his son, Matt, who was playing on the team, suggested that we might enjoy watching. Well, why not? I admit to having felt little excitement at the prospect. How could a small town slow-pitch softball tournament bring pleasure to a guy who can watch major league baseball on cable any day of the week? However, Edith enjoys new experiences, frequently pulling me out of my rut, and more often despairing at my intransigence and taking on the adventure by herself. This time I came along.

We left the boat quietly in her slip, telltales fluttering in a gentle breeze. We climbed the hill, crossed the empty main drag, and followed the sound of cheering to the softball fields. Already I thought this a good idea. The vast collection of various people and the varicolored teams on the field waiting to play reminded me of the soccer tournaments I used to attend with my son.

We found a place at the men's field, on the edge of the bleachers along the left foul line, in front of the hot-dog stand. We settled in, watched the muscular group of young men in shorts and T-shirts warm up, and shortly they were on the field.

It was fun to watch. The ball was struck almost every other pitch by young men whose workdays were spent lifting heavy objects and pulling on stubborn machinery controls and whose summer evenings were spent doing precisely this, blasting a softball into the summer sky.

After a couple of innings I noticed that the better hitters made the most outs. Matt batted without firmly setting his feet in the box. He dumped balls over the infield and short of the outfield. I do not recall him ever being put out. But the better hitters set their feet firmly in the box, watched the descending pitch, and then blasted it as hard and far as they could, the ball ascending well over the tree line, arcing high across the sky, descending way out there in the back forty.

But in the outfield are three other young, muscled men who pull levers and lift heavy objects by day and who chase down descending softballs by night. At the boom of the bat they were off dancing across the field, converging on what had seemed an uncatchable rocket, frequently one calling the other off, the ball settling in the glove, the body braced in a sudden stop and then uncoiled, the ball now arcing back into the infield.

I asked Matt about that between innings. I pointed out that when a player really slammed the ball, he was invariably out. "Yeah," Matt said, "They know that. I don't think they can help themselves."

I can understand. Without those stupendous outs, half of the ballet would have been gone from the game.

I once consulted to a company whose product was sewn together. In an attempt to better understand how the company worked, I visited a production facility. Since most of their factories were located in rural areas, I waited until I happened to be traveling through a small town in which one was located. Since as a consultant I feel a need to prove myself intelligent, I commented to the plant manager on the sewing machines arranged in groups of six so that the women at the machines faced each other. I suggested that the whole layout might be more efficient in straight lines.

"Suppose so," he said. "You see, these women are remarkable workers. Our rural production shops outperform the ones in the city. But these women don't come here to work. They come here to talk. They don't need the check that bad. Most of them are farm wives. There is work on the farm, just nobody to talk to. I line these machines up so they can't talk and they will quit. It wouldn't be fun anymore."

· One day I asked a friend of mine how business was going. He said that he had had a bad month because he had forgotten that business was a parlor game. This same man one day exploded from his office, complaining, "I have just finished watching a videotape on one of the most exciting technological breakthroughs of this decade. It was boring. Why do we have to make everything dull?"

On the human level I think it has always been important that business be fun. When I worked as a construction laborer and as a ditch digger, we were always trying to make that most tedious work into fun.

I think that dancing at work is not just about having fun. The world of business is moving too fast for the straight-line strategist. Technology shifts. Competitors enter the market copying what made a company successful yesterday. New markets are created, sometimes with the change of politics in a country whose name most of us cannot spell. Shift falls on shift daily.

In business, we once played football with time to plan in the huddles, time to look over the defense and reset the play when we came to the line. Now we play basketball, never sure from one end of the court to the other what the opposition will do. It is a different game.

In this year's NBA championships I saw Michael Jordon drive for a lay-up. He came down the right side of the free throw lane, rose in the air, began a normal right handed lay-up, and then, at the last second, transferred the ball to his left hand, reached under the basket, spun the ball against the backboard, and spun it in. A remarkable shot. Even more remarkable is that he did not have to do it that way. Nobody was guarding him! His opponent had been left behind. I think he made the lay-up the hard way because it was fun. I also think that he is one of the greatest players in basketball because he is having fun.

Edith and I left the softball field before the final game. The marina team was in it, but we felt called back to the boat to unroll the sleeping bags and prepare for the night. The next day we did inquire and found out that the marina team had indeed been the champions. That did not seem important.

What did seem important were the glorious flows and arcs of the game.

PRAGMATIC LOVE

I HAVE LEARNED TO DISTRUST THE WORD *LOVE*. I HAVE heard it used often and fervently only to be followed by behavior that seemed to me most unloving. Some church people use it to describe their relationship to the priest they will fire in a year and the choir director they hope to underpay until the final judgment. The advertising world intends that I will *love* their diet cola. And the Playboy community uses the word *love* to describe the stirrings in their loins. Fortunately, the business community uses the word *love* next to never, so I only seldom have to figure out what it could possibly mean in that context.

My wife asks for reassurance of my love, and I always hesitate, wondering what the word means this time or, for that matter, what the word means at all. The other day I came up with an answer. *Love*—or, as the dictionary puts it, "ardent affection"—has meaning only when linked with forgiveness.

Forgiveness is the touchstone that distinguishes love from infatuation. I have been infatuated with several women and hope to be infatuated with more. It's pleasant, as long as I remember what is going on. I see no faults in them. Nothing annoys me. They are perfect gems. That, of course, is not true. But that is the nature of infatuation, not to see the full person. The nature of love is to see the full person, flaws as well as charms, and forgive the flaws. Not reluctantly, but swiftly, automatically. To the point where the flaws themselves become charms.

Sometimes flaws are too large to be forgiven, and then

love dies, or is never born. Some people cannot live with less than perfection, and therefore they cannot forgive, and therefore they cannot love.

The test of love is proximity and duration. Share the same bathroom, or children, or office for a few years and then tell me you love each other. Don't tell me right after the honeymoon. That is much too soon. Wait until you have been rubbed by the traits that annoy. Wait until you have forgiven your beloved seven times seventy. Then announce to me your love. Love should be declared not during the wedding ceremony but on the anniversary, and more passionately declared every year it is proven.

Something I find astonishing is the number of people loving and forgiving me. I know I make it through life because others are willing to fill in for the things I forget or screw up or can't do. I don't feel awful about that. I feel good about that. I feel so good about that that sometimes I even forgive myself, and even love myself.

You may be working in an organization or living in a family that demands perfection as a precondition to acceptance. It insists on state-of-the-art overheads, or flawless clothing, or children with perfect school records. Approval is given as a reward for perfection. If that is the case, your situation is ill-suited to the human condition. Not just because it places you in positions of tension, demands from you your very best and then finds you wanting. Not just because you find yourself playing the same game, demanding from others things they cannot produce and delighting in the pain they experience, because if you must suffer, why shouldn't they? No, your situation is ill-suited because just as this unforgiving, unloving attitude does not work for you or them as individuals, it does not work for the organization.

In a judgmental climate, people do not risk failure. Failure is the precursor of success. Edison's light bulb did not work on the first try. Nor did Bell's telephone. Madam

Curie's greatest discovery was the result of a failed experiment. The forces in the unloving, unforgiving climate would have stopped or slowed any of them. We would have had Edison's very long candle and Bell's super-strong carrier pigeon and Madam Curie's hand-knitted shawl if they had been forced to create within the confines of many corporations.

An electronic wizard's career begins when his mother praises him in childhood for taking the radio apart and forgives him for not being able to put it together again.

"Well, now," one might object, "you can't let people do whatever they want in the name of forgiveness." True enough. But I think we can go farther than we have in many organizations, with an increase rather than a decrease in productivity and quality as the result.

Native Americans have the habit of showing up for an appointment only when they have finished whatever they were doing before. This normative behavior has had centuries of support. It is rooted in the insight that it is best to do what most needs to be done. Can you imagine an organization forgiving people for working like this and still succeeding? I consulted to a company that did. They were mostly Native Americans, so they found it easier. Any workday, if an employee had something that needed to be done, he or she could do it before coming to work or take off work to do it. However, whatever work needed to be done that day was to be done before they went home to bed. I assure you, people did not choose the late night-finish casually.

Because of this willingness to absolve people for their sick children, their flooded carburetors, and their dental appointments, this company was quite successful working with a population that others considered unemployable, until its major customer reneged on several promised large contracts. (As I said to the CEO, "White man speaks with forked tongue." But that is another essay.) My point here is that they ran a production shop that let people be people, so it's hard for me to understand why professionals, working in less interdependent situations, habitually show up late to pick up their children at the day-care center because their boss needed to see them and they could not tell that boss that their child was waiting. They fear, perhaps with good reason, that their organization loves them so little that it will not forgive them their human need to do what most obviously needs to be done.

I was with one of my client companies on an off-site retreat 150 miles from the cities, in the woods of northern Wisconsin. It was a critical and important meeting. In the middle of the meeting one member of the team was called by his wife. She was ill. She had even fainted a couple of times and was unable to take care of the children. Could he come home? He was new to the company and new to the area. This was his introduction to the team, his opportunity to prove himself invaluable. I wondered how they would accept his human frailty, the fact that he was not a dependable executive cog but a man worried about his wife, concerned about his children, anxious to be somewhere else.

One team member called home and found him the name of a doctor. Another asked his own wife to drop over and see what she could do for a woman she had never met. She not only dropped over but also brought one of her teenagers to babysit. A third lent him a car since he had ridden up with someone else. A fourth dug out a map and marked the route. There was no question on anybody's part about his going. I have never heard these executives use either the word *love* or the word *forgiveness*. But I watched them do both. I have great hopes for their company. I think it no coincidence that they get high marks from their customers for service.

On the other hand, I have been many a place where if the tie wasn't the right shade, the Vu-graph perfectly crafted, the answer on the tip of the tongue, the hair coiffed splendidly, the charm facile, the offender had a limited career. Ten years ago in one such organization I asked an executive what it took to get ahead, and he answered, "Presentation skills." That company has already crashed. It cared too much for the perfect posture, too little for reality.

I think my Native American friends take a more practical stance than that of mere screw-tightening. The demand that creates the facade renders the organization unpredictable.

Why is software development always behind schedule? Because the planner did not allow for potty breaks, coffee klatches, computer downtime, learning curves, hiring delays, document confusion, and programming error. Why not, when all those things happen every time? She couldn't forgive people for being human last time, and she will not forgive them this time. "We will do better," they say. But they cannot. So they are unpredictable. The schedule becomes hopelessly fouled. The product arrives months later than it would have if she had accepted that it could not be done as fast as she wanted it.

I knew a German-born program manager whose dictate to those responsible for providing the pieces was, "Draw me a PERT chart that allows for all reasonable contingencies. I do not care how long the plan runs. But I will take drastic steps if you miss the deadlines." Always on time and up to standard, he was highly valued. Perhaps because of his guttural accent, he had a reputation for toughness. But that was only his backup strategy. He loved people, flaws and all, and because of his willingness to forgive he lived in a predictable world.

Is it my imagination, influenced by my infatuation with a people and heritage I only slightly know, or am I hearing in the processes of total quality management, statistical process control, empowerment, and work-force diversity the muffled cadences of an ancient and kindly drum? Perhaps we are beginning to understand one of the secrets of the people we displaced from this land. I think that would be good—for me, for you, and for the organizations we depend on.

LOYALTY

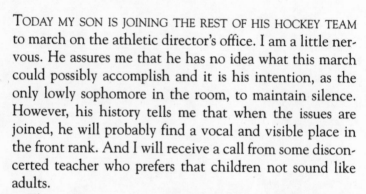

TODAY MY SON IS JOINING THE REST OF HIS HOCKEY TEAM to march on the athletic director's office. I am a little nervous. He assures me that he has no idea what this march could possibly accomplish and it is his intention, as the only lowly sophomore in the room, to maintain silence. However, his history tells me that when the issues are joined, he will probably find a vocal and visible place in the front rank. And I will receive a call from some disconcerted teacher who prefers that children not sound like adults.

They are protesting the dissolution of the Central-Highland hockey team. The state athletic board, after three years, has noticed that Central and Highland, both class AA schools, have a combined hockey team. The board has declared an end to our agreement. No matter that combining our talents has made it possible for us to win fewer than 30 percent of our games in the last three years.

At the end-of-the-year banquet, instead of hearing about last year's accomplishments and next year's hopes, these boys heard that the team that they had forged in adversity was no longer to be a team. Not because of their failure, but for some reason beyond their influence. My first piece of advice to my kid is, "Get used to it. It's going to keep happening for the rest of your life."

On my left wrist I wear a watch inscribed, "Charles W. Cowan. 30 Year Service Award. Minneapolis Gas Company." And that was not even the end of my father's career with them. He was still there when they renamed it Minnegasco ten years later. Now termination notices are given long before thirty years. Shrewd people jump corporations and make a few bucks more somewhere else. The idea of loyalty to a corporation or an employee is rapidly becoming passé.

So what is my advice to my son? Become absorbed in your own world? Feather your nest? Emotionally distance yourself from those who temporarily are wearing the same uniform? Don't pass, shoot? Build up your own stats? Look forward to becoming a free agent?

At the reunion of the Minnesota Roman Catholic ordination class of 1961, I asked those who remained in parish ministry how they survived in a church in turmoil. My friend Fred said, "I am in a small country parish. I love my parishioners. They love me. I do good work. I let God worry about the church." Wisdom comes naturally to the son of a farm-implement dealer.

I will offer Fred's advice for living in this transitory world to my son. "Love them, do good work, and hope they will love you." Let God or the market forces take care of the corporation. It won't make the separations less painful, but it will make work life more human, joyful, and productive. Anything is better than marking time, hiding from the falling ax, playing dead, bewailing assumed and actual executive errors. I know. I have done that.

Perhaps someday my son will be given the authority to match his inclination for leadership. In preparation for that day, I will tell him that the service-award watch was given to my father in 1966. It is still ticking fine twenty-four years later. For his loyalty the gas company gave my father a fitting symbol of gratitude. And for their loyalty he gave them his entire life. Not a bad deal for either of them. At least that is what he always said.

I will tell my son that there are people out there who will give him their life for an excellent watch and membership on a lasting team. Don't blow the deal if you can help it.

ON BEING A
HOCKEY FATHER

SO THERE I AM, ON THE TOP STEP OF THE STANDS, MY forehead pressed against the concrete wall, muttering imprecations. Number eight has failed. Phalen's star center has just powered by him to score what will most likely be the winning goal. So there I am, muttering imprecations at the play of some other dad's kid.

I wasn't always that way. There was a time I prevented Benjamin, my eldest son, from playing kids' hockey. But when he was in the fourth grade, I changed my mind. Most kids had been skating for four years already and if he wanted to play, it was evident he must start now or be left behind. From the first practice something changed in my life. The banging of the sticks, the skreel of the whistles, the shouts of the coaches, and those bodies hurling along the ice all invoked my fatherly pride, raised my blood pressure, and rattled my cage. And now, as my son enters his fourth year, I am hooked. Hooked to the point where a few weeks ago he had to say, "Calm down, Dad, it's just a kid's game."

Now that I am a consultant, I am given the privilege of seeing the workings of corporations from the sidelines. I am paid to be a calm and objective reviewer of the hectic activities of others. And that is what I do. I write down in cool and clinical language the passions, joys, and angers. I insert the clarifying comment. I produce the psychological model that explains the bewildering flurry of team behavior. I dispassionately ask others how they feel and what leads them to feel it.

But I remember what it felt like really to be there. I remember relishing the sense of power as others were forced to turn to me because I controlled a particular budget. I remember the paranoia about the maneuvering of others. I remember the tension of presenting to the CEO and his staff. I remember the rage at the person who failed to deliver what was promised. I remember the grumbling at my boss's inadequacies. I remember myself frequently being an emotional idiot, totally caught up in delivering my product on time and on budget and, if necessary, over the dead bodies of the rest of the world.

So why do I remain a hockey father? Why not drop the kid at the door and return to the comfort and calm of my fireplace? Because sometimes it comes together right.

My son is a graceful blue jersey breaking out from behind his own net. The opposing wings seal off the boards. He turns down the middle of the rink. He surveys the situation. And then he accelerates. Forwards attempt to catch him, but now he is moving away at a speed they did not know he had. Their defense is frantically backing up. His own wings, sensing the kill, are racing to join the play. Still accelerating, he crosses their blue line, locks his legs in a stable glide, and leans against the checking defense. He closes on the goal, a much bigger opponent draped over his back, and fires a low, firm shot. The goalie stretches, turns his padded leg, and it's a save. But no, from the side comes another flash of blue. The puck is tossed into the top of the net. It's a goal. And the five blue uniformed boys dance, congratulating one another.

There is the lure of corporate life. That moment when the product appears or the service is rendered and we can step back and say, We did it! The research is done, the concept developed, the budget prepared, the timeline laid out, the year's worth of patient steps, the revisions, the pilot testing, the revisions, the executive review, the revisions, the distribution network prepared, the sales, the delivery, the customer satisfaction. And we are the team that did it. Us, together! And under the pressure we performed better than even we thought we could.

Is it worth the bumps and bruises? After a game my son said to me, "Did you see that guy nail me? I must have flown ten feet." I saw it all right, and remember him twisting on the ice, flailing with his stick in a vain attempt to at least slash an ankle in return. But now it's a fun memory of being outplayed by a worthy opponent, as vivid as the memories of outplaying other opponents. It reminds me of my trip down the East Coast after the first productivity seminar I ran. At one office after another I took my lumps for having mismanaged the event. When appropriate I slashed back, for my accusers had conspired in the disaster. But most of the time I just bounced. They were right. I was the manager, and I had screwed it up. Funny, I enjoy the memory of that trip as much as some of the successes.

And how about the fact that business frequently unleashes in me characteristics that I have never seen described as integral to being a Christian gentleman? Well, the characteristics are useful if employed to a degree. I try to keep my checks clean, and slash only in retaliation. But I find that being willing to hit gives me some skating room.

And when my feelings get out of hand, my paranoia too high, my determination too grim, my elbows up too quickly, I hope someone reminds me, "Cool down, John, business is only a game." Then I'll put my head against the concrete wall, mutter a few imprecations in service to my overzealous heart, and when I pass number eight's father, I'll say, "Good game. Your kid was really hustling out there." And he was. There is no shame in being beaten by Phalen's star center. I hope number eight cherishes the memory of straining to catch him. It will be useful ten years from now when he joins us in the game of business. Probably as useful as having made the perfect play.

ANOTHER SON

THE PHRASE *ANOTHER SON*, IRONICALLY, WAS USED BY MY oldest son, Benjamin, to apply to himself at a time when he was left out. My younger son and I grocery shopped together when he was about four, and the clerk gave him a sucker. When Benjamin found out about this gift, he expressed his feelings of torment by saying, "Didn't you tell her that you had another son?"

Benjamin—the natural born athlete, hockey player extraordinaire, confronter of coaches and teachers, grace on the baseball diamond—has marched across these pages in all his glory more than once. I am proud of Benjamin. But I have another son, and his name is David. I am equally proud of him, for quite different reasons.

If easy athletic talent is to come to David, it has not yet arrived. His forays into the world of athletics have been social adventures in which he made many friends and batted ninth. Nor was he slow to pick up on what was happening. He hated the knowledge that easy stardom was not to be his. But he accepted it at age eight, nine, and ten. Now, at fourteen, he does not discuss it.

He has accomplished one quite physical thing, however. He is a first-degree black belt in tae kwon do. He is willing to repeat and repeat and repeat until he gets it very right. Make no mistake, he is a real black belt. At thirteen he faced his black belt review committee alongside a young man six years older than he and exhibited more knowledge and equal skill. He has put his foot and hands through boards twenty or thirty times and through a cement block once. His sparring partners know that they are in a fight when they face him.

But that is not the major source of my pride. No, it is some very small things that I am most proud about.

His black-belt committee review was a painful experience. He was asked stupid questions and expected to respond with intelligent answers. He was required to demonstrate every complex maneuver he had learned over the last four years. The stress was tremendous. He did pass. That evening he sat at the dining-room table and turned out in wrathful concentration several multicolored symmetrical designs freehand. He had never done that before and has not since. He went to bed close to tears. I asked him the next morning what he had learned from the experience. He said, "I care too much what people think. I am going to stop doing that!" I do believe he did.

After grade school he chose a different junior high school than his friends chose because he had decided it was time to change his image. I still do not know from what to what. But I know he did it. And after two years he is still in contact with his old friends despite the awkwardness of attending different schools, and he has new friends in the new school despite having to break into existing cliques.

He is a magician. He moves things from one hand to the other, and I can't tell how it was done from three feet away. He is a storyteller. My wife, a lover of storytellers, brought him as an eight-year-old to a conference of storytellers and was astounded the evening he took the microphone and told a story to this group of professionals.

But no, not yet have I centered on the deepest reason for my pride. It is a rare trait not easily named. Perhaps seeing him play cards with an old lady, joyfully oblivious to the difference in age, indicates this trait. Or when a friend of mine asked him to be acolyte at her ordination, something no sane child, including him, really wants to do, and he said that he would "consider it a privilege."

I can think of one time that captures that trait almost perfectly. He was ten. We were down at Lake Pepin and he was running across the marina parking lot. He stopped to let a five-year-old pass in front of him. And for several moments he set aside whatever he had been intent upon doing and watched that child's meanderings with interest.

As I say, I have another son. His name is David. And of him also I am quite proud. I think it unwise to canonize a fourteen-year-old. I frequently experience quite ordinary rage at his quite ordinary adolescence. But I have hints that God has given me a son who has eyes that see beneath the surface. In a sometimes blind world that is a gift indeed!

I published this essay in my own newsletter, my contact with my business world. I was astonished at the favorable response I received. People called and wrote to say how pleased they were that I had seen my own son. They told me of children of their own who they were trying to see and honor as deserved. I was pleased to receive their plaudits, even though I apparently failed to make my point.

I have no difficulty seeing David. I have difficulty seeing the security guard, the receptionist, the person in the next office, the cab driver, the hotel clerk. I am pleased that David sees people I fail to see. I pray that he continues. I have learned from him. I would like others to do so too.

TWO-FOOT-ITIS

I HAVE BOUGHT A NEW BOAT. IT IS TWO FEET SHORTER than my previous boat. It has other distinguishing characteristics, but of this one I am most proud. In the world of sailboats, there is a disease known as "two-foot-itis." First-time boat buyers live in contentment with the new boat for only a couple of years, five at the very most. Then they realize that this boat, which was the darling of their eye only a little while ago, is definitely too small for comfortable living and stout sailing. Since the governing dimension in sailboats is the length, and all other dimensions geometrically increase with the increase of the length, this realization of inadequacy is translated into a new dream, a dream of the truly proper boat, a boat *two feet* longer.

No, the normal sailor does not seek a boat four feet longer or six feet longer. The normal sailor seeks a boat two feet longer. Two to five years from the point of that purchase a boat two feet longer than that will be bought, and so on, until the boat is too long to be sailed by the number of people the sailor can coerce aboard or the sailor is too busy to sail.

This time arrives sooner than you might think. First of all, since size and complexity are increasing geometrically, price is increasing exponentially. This means the sailor is too busy working to pay for the boat to have time to sail it. And when he does have time, something is broken and must be repaired, the parts for which cost a mint, and the access to which is a claustrophobia-inducing tunnel in the bowels of the boat. So instead of sailing, the ex-sailor labors long hours at the office so that he can snatch a few moments every two weeks to lie on his back in the bilge. Not exactly the original dream, but by this time he is too busy to remember what the original dream was.

While some people, heroes all, never succumb to the urge to buy that second boat, I am the only person I know who has ever bought a boat two feet shorter than his former boat. As a matter of fact, my wife, when presented with the choice between a new twenty-five and a new twenty-three, immediately concurred that the shorter boat was obviously the right choice. Because it was what we wanted.

The *Laughing Buddha* sails like a dream. One person can handle her. There is no galley taking up room below, so she is quite spacious for a little boat. She can be trailered up to Lake Superior for an adventure or left on Pepin for friendly sailing. Three women I know who have been intimidated by larger boats are clamoring for a chance to take this one out on their own. There are forty gadgets that are not on her, that will therefore never break, and that therefore I will never pay to replace. Yet she has six brass opening ports, teak all over the place, comfortable sleeping for three, a self-tacking working jib, a forward hatch, and reading lamps. I have sailed it on its beam in a thirty-knot gust, and I have blasted across the lake in a five-knot calm. The *Laughing Buddha* has everything I want and nothing extra. That, to me, is the definition of elegance: "*Everything I want. And nothing extra.*"

Now, don't get me wrong. I am not a minimalist. Some people want a forty-foot boat, and I think that they should buy one if they can. Or work to earn the money to buy one if they can't afford it right now. The *Laughing Buddha* cost five times the old boat's trade-in value. My anxiety level has risen as I have incurred the new debt. But I am willing to pay this price for this reward. I do not want to pay a higher price for something I don't want.

Do you find yourself facing the same riddles? Tempted to buy a bigger house, although the one you have is fine and a new one will take too much of your money and energy? Tempted to climb the career ladder even though the job you have is fun and the next one is boring? Or tempted to stay in a rut because you are afraid of the risk of climbing out of it? Afraid to define what you want because then you will know that you don't have it?

Although I am one of the best people I know at resisting the herd instinct (twelve years in a monastic environment contemplating the meaning of existence should have had some effect), I still don't find it easy. I keep getting lost from my path and forgetful of my goals. When I get most down on myself, I usually wake up to the realization that I have been measuring myself with someone else's yardstick. In order to accomplish my own goals, I must measure myself on my own standards, fill my own needs. I must have quiet time for reflection on what I am trying to do. I need to respond to thought-provoking questions about who I am and who I want to become. I need to test my direction in dialogue with other people trying to live elegant lives. I need to think through how I will stay on course in an environment dedicated to pulling me off course.

No, living an elegant life is not easy. But I hate riding. Give me the tiller every time. I want to steer. That way I will have led my life, not somebody else's. Paid my costs, not somebody else's. And extracted my pleasures, not somebody else's.

BELIEF AND PRACTICE

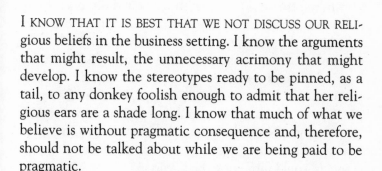

I KNOW THAT IT IS BEST THAT WE NOT DISCUSS OUR RELI-
gious beliefs in the business setting. I know the arguments
that might result, the unnecessary acrimony that might
develop. I know the stereotypes ready to be pinned, as a
tail, to any donkey foolish enough to admit that her religious ears are a shade long. I know that much of what we
believe is without pragmatic consequence and, therefore,
should not be talked about while we are being paid to be
pragmatic.

And yet one thing I believe has the deepest effect on
my business behavior. So this time I will set aside some
normal cautions and discuss the absolute center of my
religious belief.

After spending twelve years in a seminary and eight
years in the parish priesthood, I left for a number of reasons unrelated to my beliefs—the need for wife, family,
job excitement, and money. Yet within a year of going to
work with Honeywell, I redefined myself as either an
atheist or an agnostic. I do not know what happened, but
it was clear to me I no longer believed.

I had never been the type of religious fish that accepts
the hook, the line, and the sinker. I had always been a bit
of a nuisance to my seminary professors as a source of
questions to which there were no ready answers. I had
always exercised some discretion about saying what I
really believed in places where it could cause the type of
consternation I might find painful. However, my early
doubts and cynicism had always been about the edges of

faith. At the time of life I am now speaking about, I no longer believed the center.

Flat.
　　Dead.
　　　　Over.

Four or five years passed. I began to notice a phenomenon in me that did not fit with my stated disbelief. I was always sure that things would come out right. No matter how bleak the scene, no matter how contentious the participants, no matter how imminent the disaster, in my heart of hearts I remained optimistic. Not that I thought the answer would miraculously emerge, but that if we people kept at it, the answer would emerge from our collective wisdom. Not that I thought I would get the most obvious fortunate outcome, but that whatever the outcome, it would turn out to be fortunate.

But why did I expect this? It made no sense for either an agnostic or an atheist to expect it. I was forced to think through my position and realize that I believed that all of us are caught up in a creative force that is determined to do the good.

The more I affirmed that belief, the more it informed my practice. I, who am quite impatient, began waiting patiently for the process to work. I, who am quite enamored of my own intelligence, began to listen for the truth I had not grasped to be spoken by people I had not valued. I, who am quick to take offense, began to hesitate to define anyone as my enemy. I did not become perfect in aligning belief and practice, as my friends know, but I became much better.

I also began to allow my practice to inform my belief. If I did nothing different because of a religious tenet, I would not bother to argue for it, differentiate myself from others because of it, or even carry it in the intellectual satchel of my beliefs. I gave up much effort. For instance, I will not debate being Trinitarian versus being Unitarian with anyone, on or off company time. I have no idea what difference in practice a different outcome of that belief will make.

Because of what I believed, I became a churchman again. I find that being present at the weekly enactments of my tradition gives me what my friend Dick Leider calls "wake up calls." Not that many in my church believe precisely what I do, but we are close enough for friendship and dialogue. And that is all that we require of one another. And that is good, because the theological tradition I belong to has always been on the losing side of the official arguments.

Since my belief has very practical consequences, I wrote a book about it, titled *Good News for Sinners and Startravelers*. I submitted it to AMACOM because they had published my last book. The editor loved it, but he could not publish it because it was a "religious book" and his was a business press. I submitted it to Seabury Press. They thought it a good book but one that required vigorous editing to remove the business jargon. I reread the book and could find little business jargon, which proved only that I am too much of a businessman to recognize business jargon. I think that's how people talk. Seabury was too much a religious press to print my book.

Good News and I have slid through a crack in the publishing world. I say this without anger. Neither Seabury or AMACOM are in charge of ensuring a crackless world.

Now that I think about it, this crack-falling has always been the case with me.

When I was in seventh grade, I auditioned for "Catechism Comes to Life," a panel radio show featuring smart parochial school kids discussing religion with Father Louis Gales. I came out tops in the auditions, over fifteen other kids from around the cities. During the audition I told the audience what I really believed, thought, felt, and practiced. There was laughter, cheers, and applause. Nobody else got anything like the acclaim I received. I was talking to my mother a few years ago, recalling the incident. I asked her about my vague memory that at the start of the audition, after everyone else had been called by name, I had responded to the question "Is there anyone whose name I have not called?"

She knew about that. It seems that I had made a mistake in going to the auditions. Sister Ustelle, my teacher, had never intended to send me. I did not know my catechism well enough.

I never appeared on "Catechism Comes to Life." The second, third, and fourth place winners did. Apparently, the judges could not deny the acclaim, but they sure knew my ideas were not what they had in mind. They wanted the catechism to come to life yet remain orthodox. I have never seen anything both alive and orthodox.

Perhaps I have discovered a crack in the universe and am about to either fall through it or help plug it.

I am now on the lookout for friends who are interested in integrating belief and practice. I have already found quite a few. They are people who know what they believe. They don't have their beliefs because someone else gave them a list of what to believe. They are people who build their lives around their beliefs. Their everyday actions give voice to what they believe. They test everything against their picture of the universe and take the risk of choosing what they feel is right behavior and rejecting what they think is wrong.

I am on the lookout for people like these because I find them exciting, vital, worthwhile. I am on the lookout for them because they make a difference. I am on the lookout for them because if we hold hands, perhaps we will not slip through that crack in the universe—the crack between belief and practice.

Perhaps together, in this our day, we will do something quite extraordinary.

ORGANIZATIONAL SURVIVAL SKILLS FOR INNOVATIVE PEOPLE

THIS ESSAY IS WRITTEN SO THAT A FEW PEOPLE CAN redirect their own emphasis and make themselves and everybody else much happier. It is for the innovative person. You are not many, but your impact is large. To discover whether you are one, see if the following applies to you.

What does it take to be an innovative person?

a) If you are successful in innovation, you are enormously self-willed. The value in this characteristic is that you, because of your innovative ideas, are likely to receive little support from others and much negative comment. A self-willed person is more likely to carry ideas to fruition. Someone who values others and their opinions is more easily dragged to a halt.

b) You can leap ahead of most people. You add two and two and discern that if you continue, you will inevitably reach one hundred. The innovator leaps to 100 now, well ahead of more methodical minds who often do not see even the possibility of the conclusion, much less its inevitability.

c) Risk is of little concern. One hundred may not be the right answer, but you will take a chance. Further, since you are self-willed, even if the answer is not quite one hundred, you will make that the right answer. You tend not to ask others to grade you; you grade others. You are secure in your own skills, certain that even after a failure others will value you.

d) You do not tolerate nonsense. You are reality-oriented. You cut through red tape, foibles, and weaknesses with a viciousness born of the need to protect your own ties to the bedrock of reality, ties that make you what you are.

So why do you have trouble surviving happily in organizations, or why do others have trouble surviving with you? To understand this you must understand what it takes to nurture an organization.

a) The nurturing person must be attentive to the needs of others, willing to sacrifice his own will to the will of the whole. Since organization members whose needs are not met sometimes get out and often turn off, organizations need compromisers more than they need stubborn innovators.

b) The nurturing person lets others think through things for themselves. She is attempting to grow others. If she has an innovative thought, she may choose to repress it. Innovation is not an essential part of the task of the nurturing executive; developing commitment and thoughtfulness in others is.

c) The nurturing person tries to reduce risk for others. He knows that everyone is not gifted; everyone cannot afford to start over fresh tomorrow. Most people need security, and he provides it so that they may work without fear of losing their paycheck or their dignity.

d) "Nonsense" is a way of organizational life. Add together the foibles of a large number of people and some laughable, inefficient, non–reality-oriented ways of doing business emerge. Although this person trims the nonsense, she is shrewd enough to allow and laugh off much. Although not pretentious, she will allow some pretensions in others if it provides for their needs and advances the organization.

The innovator is not well designed to nurture an organization. You cause pain and experience frustration. If you do not want to change the way you are, or are incapable of doing so, here are five rules for surviving your own genius that will make life a little easier for everyone:

1. Pay attention to what is going on already in your organization. Before plowing ground, make certain that other people have not already planted seeds there, which will grow to perfectly serviceable plants if you leave them alone. Plow under another person's work only when you are certain the gains will be immense.

2. If you are a chief executive, hire someone else to run the show. You may want someone who never had an original idea but does an excellent job of understanding and valuing the ideas of others—even yours!

3. If you are a member of an organization, remember that by your very existence you are a challenge to the self-worth of your colleagues and management. Do not make matters worse by putting them down, showing up their lacks. They may score low on creativity, but how do you score on decency, or on methodicalness, or on helpfulness, or practicality?

4. Tolerate the fact that most people will only approximate doing what you know needs to be done. If they were all as radically creative as you, you would not be valued as highly as you are now. Live with the fact that they do not have your vision. Do not expect them to live up to your standards in this matter and perhaps they will forgive you your faults in other areas.

5. Run for daylight. Do not apply your energies to what other people are already trying to do. Although most people fear vacuums, the vacuum is your natural ele-

ment. Apply your energies to them. Everyone will love you for it.

There are others better able to take on much of the work of the organization. Value them as they value you. Your capacity to get done what you want to get done will improve. Instead of recalcitrant bitterness and anger, you will engender in others supportive friendship and respect.

Without you the organization will be a dull, uncreative place. But a sad fact of life is that without you they can do a great deal better than you can do without them.

WHO GOES THERE?
CHARACTER AND PARTICIPATIVE
MANAGEMENT

MY THINKING ON THE RELATIONSHIP BETWEEN CHARAC-
ter and participative management began when I was reading Peter Drucker's autobiography. I was enchanted with
the beginning, excited by the middle, and bored by the
end. Drucker did not change. He was as insightful at the
finish as he had been at the opening gun. No, it was not
Drucker who had changed. It was the people he was writing about.

First he enchanted me with his stories of the European
statesmen with whom he had been as a child and a young
man. Next he excited me with stories of intuitive businessmen with whom he had worked early in his career,
people who made brilliant business decisions based on few
facts and much wisdom. And then he bored me by
explaining the ponderous business strategies of modern
corporate giants. The first two groups had character, the
third avoided having character in plodding pursuit of success through massive mediocrity.

Drucker told of the retired businessman who sold the
last of his stock in the department-store chain he had created when he discovered that the dress department did
not carry his wife's size. In his opinion, a well-managed
store would. He was right. In a couple of years the store
faltered because of poor management. He told of the
international financier who backed away from a deal
because the promoter presenting the opportunity knew

the answers to all the financier's questions. In the financier's judgment, honest men seldom know all the answers. He was right. The promoter was a crook.

Can an organization devoid of characters such as these remain successful in the long run? After years of working in a bureaucracy, I am convinced that the absence of character is the cancer of organizations.

It's the little people who aren't there who are killing us. An executive I know commented on the number of intelligent people he had hired to be asleep at the switch. Another brilliant prober into the workings of his organization wonders that no one else ever asks the questions he asks. It is people of character who throw the switch; it is people of character who ask probing questions. The organization that does not encourage character would do better to replace its people with microchips. They have no character either, but they are less expensive and more reliable.

And what does participative management have to do with character? Participative management is in a position to reduce the amount of character in an organization.

When I first started in this business, the boys in the line, my trainees, were always worrying that participative management might lead to "group think," and I was always assuring them they had it wrong—this was the seedbed of individual opinion. Now I think we were both right.

The culture organization development professionals intend to create allows all to be themselves, at least within reasonable limits. But the techniques we use burr off people's rough edges, and frequently those rough edges are essential ingredients in the overall recipe for character. We teach the perfectionist patience with others, and he stops demanding the best. We teach the creative genius to respect the slowness with which a group learns, and she stops sharing her unorthodox leaps. We teach the ogre of operations that fear is an unseemly emotion and do not understand as the factory meanders out of control. We intend to moderate, but instead we debilitate.

Why must character bend to mediocrity? Cannot mediocrity become character?

The first step is this: Reunite people with their histories. Help them rejoice in their ethnic origins. Let them tell you what their college was trying to teach them about being a person. Encourage reflection on the kind of people their parents and grandparents were. Ask them what kind of person joins their church. Ask for stories about the manager who taught them the most. Let them know that it is legitimate in this organization to be an individual.

Character is waiting to emerge. The reason it does not is that we have not allowed one another our histories, our ethnic origins, our colleges, our churches. We have implicitly told one another that the corporate person exists without these. We have told one another that there is an instant corporate character that will be handed out along with ID cards.

But there is no such thing as instant character. How can we expect deep pools of character if people are disconnected from the long streams of personal tradition?

There is more to be done beyond the first step:

•Focus less on diminishing the powerful and more on why the powerless have given away their power.

I have been invited to consult to many managers who were overwhelming those who reported to them. "He is a bull in the china shop," those who hired me would say. "Do what you can to fix him." Time after time I found a person who was ignorant of the terror he was causing. Usually he was a person of intensity and intelligence, to whom no signals were being given of his negative effects. My first step is to confront him with the untold feelings of those around him. Frequently that is more than enough to tilt him to a different path. My second step is to ask those around him why they were afraid to talk to him directly, to take him on. Usually I discover that they are unwilling to risk anything, even telling their boss in a straightforward manner that they do not like being shouted at. People who are unwilling to take risks will never have impact. People who are unwilling to lose will never gain. This should not be a new message, but to many, it is. It begins in school where docility is rewarded with good marks, and it ends in the large bureaucracies where anonymous performance is rewarded with raises. It is time for a new message. Take risks, or others will push you around. Sorry about that, Charlie, but that's the way it works.

•Focus less on burring off the rough edges, and more on living with idiosyncrasies.

In one of my client systems the human resource people frequently tell me that Max's vice presidents are afraid of him and so they seldom challenge him in meetings. This comment is usually passed on with a reproachful expression. They feel that in my work with Max I should have changed all that. My work has been effective, and Max has changed quite a bit. But what his reports now understand is that Max is a deep-thinking introvert, not a fast-thinking extrovert. Challenge him in a meeting and he can't keep up; he turns mulish. They know it. Max knows it. When they see him locking in, they drop the topic and pick it up a day later in a one-on-one meeting where Max can think. Their willingness to let the boss be himself keeps them out of unproductive jams, and leads to well-thought-out solutions.

•Focus less on generic interpersonal skills and more on skills that work for a particular individual with a unique character.

I would never suggest to a dominating, highly verbal person that she get openly angry in dealing with others. I would suggest it to a quiet, kindly, and compassionate woman. In the first instance, the anger would be too much; people would say that she is really going overboard. In the second instance, most people would say that if *she* popped her cork, things must have gotten really bad. Courses in interpersonal skills frequently come from the manuals developed by academic psychologists who hope to reform the masses. I don't have much faith in them. There are too many individual differences in people to begin to prescribe one way of doing anything.

My experience has been that it is the people of intricate and complex character who move organizations forward. In our efforts to lift up the weak, in many cases we have enfeebled the strong. It is not necessary. Everyone can be strong. I think it time that we work together in our organizations to decrease the odds that the answer to the question "Who goes there?" is "Nobody."

HANK, AN UNLIKELY SAINT

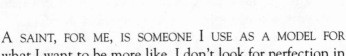

A SAINT, FOR ME, IS SOMEONE I USE AS A MODEL FOR what I want to be more like. I don't look for perfection in my saints—just qualities that I find admirable and imitable.

I must first say that Hank did not like me a lot. He didn't even like me a little. As a mutual friend put it, "John, you will never get ahead in an organization managed by Hank." I asked what hint he had picked up that told him so. "Hank said it. It's a direct quote." So it will come as no surprise that Hank and I were not close. What I have to tell you about him is based on glimpses and hearsay. I haven't even heard his name mentioned in the last three years. I, however, have used his name often and all over the place. I think he would resent the number of times I've quoted him or told someone how he would have responded to a situation or suggested one of his management principles to a client as a useful norm to follow. You see, I think Hank is a saint.

But he is an unlikely saint. Lots of people did not like him. "He is hard on people," they would say. "He shouts at meetings. He blusters. He demeans people." And I guess that is more or less true. I never actually saw it happen. I saw things that were close enough to it that I remained nervous in his presence.

So why do I want to canonize him? I'll tell you a few stories, and then I will tell you why.

I was leading a meeting at which he was a guest. Given his opportunity on the agenda to speak, he turned to the vice president of the most profitable division in the corporation and asked, "Why does the receptionist at your Maryland facility have time to knit?"

To which the vice president responded, "I don't know."

That might not seem a brilliant response, and it did earn him thirty seconds of Hank's contemptuous silence, but consider the options. If he had said that he did not know that the receptionist knitted, Hank would have suggested that if Hank knew she knitted, the division vice president should know she knitted. If he had said that it was unimportant that she knitted, Hank would have pointed out that if the most visible person in the whole division knitted, what was going on in the corners where people could hide? And if he had suggested that as an executive he had bigger fish to fry, Hank would have asked him how can an executive focus on anything more important than making sure that people have useful work to do?

Now you might think from this that Hank was a slave driver. That is not so. We ran productivity questions in the annual employee-attitude survey. One question was, "Do you have enough work to do?" Hank's organization was the only one in the corporation with a perfect bell curve from too much to too little. Every other organization was skewed to one side or the other.

I once screwed up a seminar some of Hank's people had attended. That night, a Thursday, they flew to the East Coast. My boss had a call on his desk from Hank at 8:30 Friday morning. Hank had used the hour time differential to call the participants and ask them how they had liked the seminar. I think my boss earned a couple of points by being able to tell him that he already knew it hadn't gone well and knew why. He didn't earn enough points to cause Hank to send us more participants.

Another friend of mine, Dick, a CEO of a decent-size company, tells the story of flying to Boston and finding that his seatmate was from our corporation. Dick bled all over him about the lousy service he was getting on a specialized software package he was buying. The next morning Dick got a call at his hotel. There would be a meeting that afternoon to discuss the software package. His presence was requested. The meeting was being chaired by his seatmate from yesterday's flight, the group vice president to whom this subsidiary reported. His name, of course, was Hank. Who else would do that?

When I was managing, one of my people, Joanne, after spending thirty minutes trying to explain a data-base problem to me, said, "If you will get off of your bottom and walk into the next room, I can show you what happens on the screen." She was right, and I so hated to do it. I was a manager. I liked abstractions and generalities. I didn't want to work with specifics.

And that is why I want to canonize Hank. He lived in a world of specifics, in which he learned specific things and fixed specific problems. What else is there to fix? How do you fix a generality or an abstraction? I don't know. But I have watched a lot of people try to do it.

So, for a model executive, I give you Saint Hank, the saint of the specific question and the specific answer.

MOTHER'S DAY

In 1955 I was a Roman Catholic priest, an assistant pastor at Saint Anthony of Padua in northeast Minneapolis. Life was very routine and quite safe. It looked as if I could keep doing what I was doing forever. The financial rewards were not great, but I was assured a pleasant life-style until age sixty-five, honor in the community, and a fair amount of power. It was not something to tamper with idly.

One day I was bored and vaguely remembered that a program was being offered at the Catholic Youth Center that I might even have signed up for. Knowing that my roman collar opened most doors, certainly most church doors, I did not hesitate to test my welcome. By God, I had signed up! I and thirty others were seated to hear two Episcopal priests address us on "New Models of Ministry."

As I remember, it was not bad. They did not talk a lot. We played some nonverbal games and did a little role playing, and one of them gave a short presentation. It was pleasant and mildly instructive. They mentioned that they were experimenting with a new-style human-relations workshop and handed out information on how to attend. Wanting an interesting break in the tedium of summer, I signed up. I gave it little further thought until the day a couple of months later when I arrived for a four-day creative risk-taking workshop at the Hudson House in Hudson, Wisconsin.

There is no way to ease into describing this. Most people there found it an emotionally challenging experience.

Many tears were shed, many feelings voiced, many hard truths passed on. At one point somebody, in an excess of frustration, put his fist through a wall (not a very sturdy wall, but a wall nevertheless). These were the reactions of normal people.

I was not normal. I had never checked into a motel before. I had never been outside the society of my own church. I had been educated since age thirteen in a monastic male environment. For years my interaction with people had been dampened by the respect thought due a man of the cloth. Here I was, sitting on the floor, in mixed company, trying to articulate my own feelings and hearing how others felt about me—not all of it good! If normal people experienced the workshop as earthshaking, you can imagine my emotional state. I spent my days in semishock and my nights trying to fit this experience into everything else I had learned about life.

At the close of the workshop nearly everyone hugged one another as did I, but with an absence of fervor. Something was vaguely wrong. I liked these folks, but—? I was halfway home when it struck me. I was expressing love and caring for all these people, and I had never told my mother I loved her.

I must do that sometime, I thought on the way home. Perhaps I'll call her when I get to the rectory; after all, I have been gone for four days and there is work to be done. A few miles later I decided I'd call her that day, and after a few more miles, that I would call her and ask her if I could stop by. And by the time I entered the city limits, I decided maybe I'd just drive over to her house *right away*.

Driven by my feelings, I rushed through the door in tears. We sat on the sofa and wept before I even began to speak. I told her I loved her. Two years after my mother died, my sister told me that that day was one of the high points in my mother's life. As well it should be. It was a turning point in mine.

For those of us who rush through life trying to do something useful that other people will pay for, it seems to me wise not to forget to touch a few of the critical human bases. I have closed a few sales in my life, and collected a few bonuses, and been promoted, and I enjoyed and savored every one of these events. But while I know they happened, I only dimly remember them. On the other hand, I could describe to you the angle of the sun, the tilt of the blinds, and the color of her dress the day I told my mother I loved her.

Perhaps there are people deserving your phone call? Your visit? Don't skip it for business. You may be denying them a high point of their life. You may be avoiding your own most unforgettable moment.

THE BACKYARD TREE

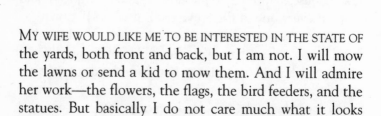

MY WIFE WOULD LIKE ME TO BE INTERESTED IN THE STATE OF the yards, both front and back, but I am not. I will mow the lawns or send a kid to mow them. And I will admire her work—the flowers, the flags, the bird feeders, and the statues. But basically I do not care much what it looks like. But from time to time, vegetation crops up that is a little too much for her to handle, and when it does, she sends me to the backyard.

About eight years ago she sent me into the backyard with a simple assignment. I was to remove a nasty little tree that somehow or other had found a niche three inches from the garage foundation and had developed to a height of about four feet. I asked her why she had not simply yanked it out, and she said that it had resisted her tugging and it was about time I did something to contribute to the yard anyway. Which was true.

So I went out to pull up the tree. It did not move. I yanked on it until it was bare of leaves, and it budged not. So I got a shovel to dig it up. Except that it did not come up. As deep as I went, I could not reach the bottom of its roots. Some of them were embedded under the garage floor, and I'll swear this is true, some of them had worked their way into the concrete itself.

I got out the ax. The roots were now exposed, and with whacks and thumps and grunts I whopped them apart. Four feet of tree I now held in my hand. It was a stick with stubby roots. I couldn't throw it away. Anything that clings to life as this tree does deserves a chance, I decided. I replanted it.

This time I gave it some room—six feet south of the deck and three feet east of the fence. I dug it a hole and stuck it in. That was all: no water, no fertilizer. Nothing.

It grew. A year later it was five feet tall. My neighbor, the ancient Mort, leaned on the fence and said, "I see you have a walnut tree there."

"The hell you say," I said. "Is that what it is?"

"Yes, a walnut tree. Those two trees on the far side of my yard are walnut trees. They are horrible trees. They leach the moisture from the yard. Grass and flowers can't grow by them, they tip up the fence, and they drop walnuts all over, some of which hit people. Those that don't, jam your mower. You might want to dig that thing up while it's still small."

"The hell you say," I said.

I did not dig it up. I pruned it some. I began to pay attention to it as I pay attention to nothing else about the yard except the height of the grass. I am a perverse fellow, I guess, and I like perverse things.

When Benjamin was six months old, my friend Vern, who is a most able behavioral psychologist, told me that I was making a mistake in the way I disciplined my child.

"The hell you say," I said.

"Right," he said. "Here is what you should be doing. When he asks for something, decide whether or not you are going to give it to him. If you are going to give it to him, give it. If not, deny him. But do not change your mind. That way he will know that arguing is useless. The way you are doing it now, he is learning to fight with you about everything he wants. You will have no peace and quiet for the next twenty years."

"Good point!" I said, but I didn't take his advice. I thought, when the kid is thirty and asks his boss for a raise and his boss says no, do I want him to be the kind of person who accepts that answer, or do I want him to be the kind of person who fights?

A couple of decades ago I was one of ten human relations trainers running one-week sensitivity-training
groups at a human-relations workshop for cops. The dean
of the laboratory stopped by to observe my group. After
an hour he asked the group if they were curious why I, the
official facilitator, was so silent. He was curious himself.

Everybody laughed. "He is silent because we told him
to shut up. We think he is in the way." A couple of hours
later they let me talk again. They decided that maybe I
was useful after all. Believe it or not, my greatest moment
of satisfaction in that laboratory, my realization that I had
won in my efforts to get these guys to talk straight about
their feelings, came at the moment they told me to be
quiet.

I like people who are alive. People who are alive are
hard to control. They have ideas, aspirations, and feelings, including anger. They are going somewhere. If I get
in their way, they try to stomp on me.

But I prefer them to nice people.

When I was a parish priest, I yelled across the street to
Mary Harrigan, "Hey, Mary, you're really a nice girl!"

And she yelled back, "Hey, Father, don't call me nice!"

Absolutely right! Mary was not a nice girl. She was
bright. She was honest. She was good. She was hard-
working. But she was not nice. If she was, she would not
have yelled back.

Nice people have the bad habit of letting me down.
Nice people don't offer me anything I have not thought of
before. Nice people don't save me from my mistakes. Nice
people end up acting on feelings they have always had but
never wanted to tell me about.

In one neighborhood we lived in, my wife and I divided
everybody into two classes, the good and the evil. Good
people said, "Our little Charlie is going through a stage,
but we are sure that with God and Dr. Spock's help we

will get him through it." Evil people said, "If Charlie does that one more time, I will knock his block off."

We avoided the good people. We congregated with the evil people and considered ourselves ranked among them.

A lot of stuff I read about empowerment makes my stomach queasy. I do not think people become empowered by someone being nice to them. Insofar as any-one can empower anyone else, they do it by treating people like people. Sometimes they are nice, sometimes not. The empowering manager is one who is one's sweaty self, sometimes secure, sometimes shaken, sometimes wise, sometimes foolish—but always willing to be in human connection with the people who work for him.

Let people experience the consequences of their own mistakes. I have never pushed my eldest son for better marks. I did remind him that students failing courses do not play hockey. He decided not to fail. And then Tony, a senior, an athlete, and a scholar, sat him down and explained to him which grade-point averages and SAT scores gain athletes scholarships. Ben raised his own sights.

Joe, when he was my boss, once refused to review a memo I had written from our department to the chief executive. He explained that once he read it, he was responsible for the contents. If he did not read it, I was responsible. I rewrote that memo three more times before I sent it. That was one good memo.

If you want to become empowered, just do it—as long as you are polite. Others will have to figure out how to deal with you.

A secretary named Ursula joined our Quality department one day. She was German-born with a thick accent. I don't know if she knew that secretaries are to be seen but not heard. "Chon, I can't read your writing. Rewrite this," she would say. "I have no time now. It is not important. I will do it when I can." "Why do I type these weekly reports when Bill throws them in the basket? Why don't you just tell him what you're doing?" We were not a particularly enlightened group. But we were all pleased to have Ursula aboard. We did not always get what we asked for. But we always knew why we were not getting it. And we always got what we needed. Ursula turned out four times as much work as the nice secretary sitting next to her, saying "sure" to everything and then letting the work sit in her in basket.

As I type this, my son Benjamin is maneuvering to get me to buy him a car. I told him I would do that for his senior year, starting in the fall. This is mid-July, and he is lining up a job to show me that he has the money to keep the car running and that he will need the car to get to the job. He is parading car deals before me from the paper, real steals that if we don't buy now may be unavailable next fall. And I am weakening. Actually, I think he is right. It is about time to buy that car. He is convincing me.

I have some confidence that in a few years a corporation will be lucky to get him as an employee. However, I may have overdone my patience with the perverse and created a lawyer.

Last night I sat on the deck in the shade of the walnut tree. Thirty feet she stretches. Her upper branches are reaching toward the lower branches of Mort's trees. I was basking in my pleasure at this, my creation when the walnut fell, one foot to my left, with a very solid thump. Yes, that could have hurt. I looked up. There are several up there waiting to drop.

Aw, well, Mort warned me.

LEARNING

NANCY AND HARVEY CAME SAILING LAST SUNDAY. THEY both rate my good-egg-of-the-year award. I called them on Saturday to tell them that the weather forecast was not favorable, with a 50 percent chance of rain and thunderstorms. Harvey asked if I would go if I were going alone. I said yes.

"Then we are coming too. After all, this is an adventure."

The two of them, both nonsailors, showed up early, with rain gear and more food than even I could eat. They asked what they could do to ready the boat for the water. We sailed in a light wind, a heavy wind, some sunshine, and rain. Once we hid in the harbor to avoid a thunderstorm. When the thunder stopped and the rain died, even though the skies were still gray, Nancy made the decision that we should go back out.

Harvey drove the boat most of the time. At first I gave him a constant stream of directions, then fewer and fewer still, until we were at the point that his judgment on the basics was nearly as good mine.

"You are low, Harv. Bring it up, bring it up. Whoops, you were right, Harv. Take it back where you had it."

"Harv is a one-time learner," Nancy said a couple of times, quite proudly. "Show him once and he has it."

She is right. I enjoy the after-image of a rain splashed Harvey skillfully guiding the *Laughing Buddha* down the lake after an hour's instruction. Of course there is more to be learned about sailing than Harvey knows now. A few hours of sailing provides only the tiniest portion of the experiences the wind and waves are willing to dish out over several years.

I had a strange realization on that trip. The wind had been blowing at a solid fifteen knots for a while, and we were racing along with everything up, Harvey at the helm. Then the wind began to increase. We were now at an uncomfortable angle of heel, sliding over on our side in the gusts. The rain was around Lake City and coming our way fast. I told Harv that it was time to take down the genoa and directed him to tack so that as I dropped the genoa from the cockpit, it would hit the deck and not the water. We executed the move perfectly.

The wind kept increasing. I would guess it was at thirty knots as I looked down the now rolling lake, whitecaps showing on half of the waves. As I shrugged into my yellow raincoat, I thought, "Got it made. We are in complete control. We won't even see a forty-knot wind with these conditions, and if we do, we are already rigged correctly to take it."

Then I realized, "This lake no longer frightens me. I know what to do, and I know I can do it."

I should have felt triumph. Instead I thought, "Maybe it's time to sell the boat."

I have sailed boats for twenty-five years off and on, keelboats for the last seven. Every time I have left the dock, I have been afraid, knowing that the lake was about to teach me something and unsure that I would prove an apt pupil. I have not been challenged every time, but enough times to know that the challenge is there. I have always survived, sometimes with skill and class, and sometimes in an embarrassing but not fatal mess. I do not think that Lake Pepin has anything up its sleeve that I have not seen and do not know how to handle. I am not cocky. I may not succeed in handling the situation, but I am fairly confident I know how.

I do not like this.

I have enjoyed learning all my life. I enjoy it more than knowing how. I teach others how to do things to force myself to learn more. I have had students tell me that a course I taught was good because they learned a lot. I remember the same course as disappointing, because I learned nothing. I did not learn much in school. I lacked experience. The wisdom of the books was poured into a vessel without a bottom. Mostly it went right through.

But once I started working, I learned a lot. There was no such thing as a dry psychology text when people were on the doorstep with problems I did not know how to solve. I read everything I could get my hands on, and I read it avidly. I find nothing more challenging than sitting for the first time with a client who intends to explain an organization to me once and expects that I will understand it.

I left the parish priesthood not because I was bad at it but because I was good at it. I could put together a passable sermon in fifteen minutes. Because I was good at it I was getting worse. Lacking challenge, I was beginning to drift.

I entered industry and spent two years in semiterror. I knew some things that most in the company didn't. That is why they hired me. They knew how to run a business, and I didn't. That is why I was terrified. And learning.

I had just begun to gain a grasp on how to be a corporate citizen when I joined a consulting firm. I nearly drowned. Every other week I was in Washington, D.C., consulting to the federal government. What a strange world it was. I never did master it, but I learned quite a bit, mostly what never to try again. Then I went back into a corporation to become a program manager. I learned about budgeting, control, power, putting together coalitions, working with divisions. After nine years there, I was pretty good at what I did and still not bored, because every three years I received a new job and a new challenge. The last time they moved me, they moved me out. I went back to consulting, being terrified, and learning again.

Years ago some friends of mine were trying to find out what kept some engineers from becoming technologically obsolescent and what allowed others to fall behind the industry and become dead weight on the corporation. One of the things they hoped to discover was that the classes they were providing on technical subjects were a big help.

The classes were not a big help. The single determining factor in an engineer's technical growth and worth to the company was the job assignments he received. If the engineer's boss thought well of him, he was given the toughest work to do. In doing it, he had to learn. When he finished the task, he had gained new knowledge, was more technically competent, and therefore was the obvious candidate for the next hard assignment.

This explained one phenomenon. At the beginning of their careers, engineers with the company for one to five years looked pretty much alike. Their skills were fairly comparable. After five years they began to fall roughly into two groups, and after ten years it was clear that some were very skilled and others were destined to be drones. The drones tended to sign up for classes in a desperate but futile attempt to break the cycle.

I have found this little piece of information very informative.

I will stay on Lake Pepin. I am comfortable with the marina. I like chatting with Joe and Sue and Neil. Dorothy's Ship's Wheel Cafe and the Parkview remain among my favorite places to eat in the world. It is the most beautiful lake I have even seen, and it's within two hours of my house. I enjoy taking my friends aboard and educating them on the art of sail. "Here is how a sail interacts with the wind," I say, and go on with the terms of the mystery: port and starboard, halyards and sheets, points of sail, rules of right-of-way. None of it is abstract.

"This rope is called a sheet. This knob is called a winch. Wrap this sheet around this winch and pull it in. See how the sail fills. Wrap the sheet on this cleat. Look how the boat is picking up speed."

Since I like teaching, I am still having fun, but I am not learning, or not learning a lot.

I still make mistakes. The other day while the *Buddha* was on autopilot and I was on the radio, the boat began to jibe and I reached up with my hand to catch the boom. It hurt. But it was not a lesson. I know better than to do that. I have learned before that the sail in a jibe starts moving with deceptive slowness and then suddenly develops painful force. I will always make mistakes. Unlike Harvey, I am not a one-time learner.

In August I am towing the boat to Bayfield for two weeks on Lake Superior. Once again, I am terrified. I will be sailing to destinations I can't see, on a lake easily capable of seven-foot waves. I will be anchoring out in pitch black without the benefit of lights from towns and cabins for reference points in the night. I plan to be away from restaurants for long periods, dependent on my one-burner alcohol stove. I will be scared silly for two weeks. But I expect that I will learn a lot.

I don't know where this force in my life will take me. Perhaps on to a really big boat sailing on the ocean. I'll wait and see. That really frightens me.

If I end up in a nursing home, I plan to have it be the one up from the harbor down at Lake Pepin. Look for me there. I am the one experimenting with the wheelchair, looking for new ways to get a little speed out of it. I am the one explaining to the new resident, "It's all in the wrists. See, grab the wheel like this and flip it like this. You get a straighter line with less effort." I might even write a book about it. If you want to do me a favor, buy it. But if you really want to learn, I suggest that you sit down in the wheelchair and try it. Save the book until later. I just reread the owner's manual for the Seaward 23'. I didn't learn anything from it the first time. Now that I have spent two summers sailing the *Buddha*, I find the manual very instructive. There is nothing like experience to whet the appetite for knowledge.

If you are not getting new experience, consider testing a bigger lake.

THE SAILING INSTRUCTOR

RUTH, MY MOTHER, TAUGHT ME ABOUT SAILING through life. She did not know how to sail a boat. She did not even know how to swim.

I bought my fifteen-year-old sister a sailboat, which we launched at the family cabin. It was twelve feet long. The top of the boat cleared the water by about four inches. My sister and I both learned to sail it. I now know that we were doing several things wrong and misunderstood some of the basic principles of sailing. Yet we did manage to make the boat go, frequently where we wanted it to, and when we capsized, the lake was warm and only four inches away. The fall did not hurt.

My mother used to go for rides with me on that boat. Since she did not swim, she wore a life preserver. She sat with her back to the mast and trusted me to keep the boat upright. Not wanting to violate that trust, I usually took her out in the evening, when the winds were light. Somehow we never got caught by a storm or even a heavy wind. I do not understand why. It happens to me often now. If it had happened then, maybe she would have died younger, because in heavy winds I frequently, inadvertently, tipped the boat over.

We would sail down to the far end of the lake, about two miles; by then the wind would be dying, barely moving the boat, and we would turn back. Then we would hear the ten-horse plowing down the lake. My father and the fishing boat would pull alongside.

"Want a tow?"

"No, thank you," she would say.

The boat became slower and slower as the wind died. There would be barely a ripple on the water and only the slightest motion to the boat. I would twist the tiller from side to side, pushing the boat ahead. My father's fishing boat would appear, the same question would be asked, the same answer given. Around sunset Mom would finally accept the tow.

On an unusually happy day I told my mother that I felt I had a song in my heart. She said that she felt that way all the time. I believed her.

On the surface she did not have an obviously happy life. We were not miserable. But we were not wealthy, and we had more than our share of internal family strife. She had enough reason to be unhappy if she chose. Still, as she said, she lived with a song in her heart.

The first principle of sailing is to keep the mast up and the keel down. The next is to tack when headed, and this great principle my mother understood despite the fact that she did not know how to sail.

A sailboat cannot sail directly into the wind. The old square riggers could not even come close. They often waited for the wind to change so that it was blowing in the direction they wanted to go. Modern sailboats do much better. There is no need to wait for the wind to change. Still, even a modern boat has difficulty sailing much closer to the wind direction than thirty degrees off of it. The *Laughing Buddha* can do that. The *Hummingbird* could barely make it to forty-five degrees off of the wind. That is why I sold her.

When a sailboat's destination is directly upwind, the sailboat sets its nose thirty degrees off the wind on one side and sails that way for some time. Then it flips the nose to the other side and sails thirty degrees off the wind in that direction. Eventually it gets to its destination. This is called "tacking," and each of the directions is called a tack.

Wind does not remain constant. It increases and dies, and it shifts from side to side. A sailboat is headed when, on a tack, the wind shifts toward the bow of the boat. Since the sails begin to flap, the sailboat is tempted to veer off a few more degrees from the destination. The odds are that a sailboat will go farther faster if it tacks when headed. Thus the principle, "When headed, tack."

I grant this is a long explanation if you are uninterested in sailing. (If you are a sailor, you recognize that it is a short and incomplete explanation.) I give it because sailing is a system in which this phenomenon is most evident. Business systems work similarly, but I am forever astounded at people in business who cannot see that they are being headed and fail to tack.

My mother understood this principle and taught it to me. She was raised a Baptist. To marry Charlie she had to become a Catholic. So she did. She gave up working to raise babies. When we were older and the family needed money, she worked. She was a legal secretary and one of the best. She worked diligently and well until she picked up the signs that she was no longer going to make financial progress at the firm, or that her talents were no longer appreciated at the level she preferred them to be appreciated. She then quit, came home and became a housewife again, until she found it boring or we needed money. And then back she went to work, usually in a better job, and frequently for the same firm that she had quit. They would notice the vacuum she had left and be eager to do anything to get her to return.

Mom was not a balloon being blown about by life, although someone who did not know her might read her concessions to the wind as weakness. She always knew where she was going, what she wanted to achieve. She never fought the wind. She tacked. But she almost always ended up precisely where she wanted to go. No wonder she had a song in her heart.

On a sailboat, when headed, the sails begin to flap and

the boat slows down. In a business, profit margins decay, sales hold constant or slip, market share is reduced, technology falls behind the competition's, customer satisfaction deteriorates. The temptation is to do more of what got the business to its original state of success. I say the first thing to do is check the wind. See what is different out there. The odds are it is time to tack. Tack to find a new market, a new product or service, or an upgrade in technology. Whenever the boat slows down, first check the wind.

For a person in an organization, some of the signs of being headed are a drastic drop in work load, a transfer to a less significant assignment, less access to the powers that be, or a less-than-average or average raise. Check the wind. It may be time to tack. That is: Find a new job, find a new boss, change your manner of operating. When you are headed, your position tends to continually worsen. You lose a few degrees and the wind shifts on top of you again, and then you lose a few more degrees. If you had tacked, you would be closer to your goals.

Management decides you can't handle the tough jobs, then it decides you can't handle the normal jobs, then it decides you can't handle any job. You could have been in a new job or a new company, gaining prestige instead of losing it.

Once I was in charge of a placement center for displaced executives. In retrospect every one of them could tell the story of being headed. The signs had been there, but they had refused to tack.

I understand it. I always experience the same reluctance on the water. The boat is tipped to one side, the sails are set and tied down, the pop cans are leaning comfortably against the seats. I know what will happen when I tack. I will untie ropes, pull on winches, retie ropes. The boat, after the noisy thrashing of sails stops, will tilt the other way. Pop cans will tip over, luggage will fall off the seats, everybody will scramble to new positions, and I will step on my sunglasses.

After the tack is complete, I will make progress again. Those executives in the placement center would have been better off seeking a new tack before their abilities were in question, before they were parked in a nothing job, and certainly before they were sent to the placement center.

My mother went to a rest home in her early seventies. She suffered from osteoporosis, and over the last few years she had been gradually losing control over her body. She doubled over, had trouble lifting her head, could not raise her voice. As she was pushed down the street in a wheelchair, her head tended to precede the chair, looking not unlike the figurehead on the bow of a ship.

I came up to the fourth floor to see her one day and the nurse at the station said to me, with a smile, "Have your mother tell you how she called the cops on us."

There was nothing wrong with Ruth's mind up to this point. But as I hurried down the hall I wondered if she had begun slipping. She told me the story in the barely audible voice that went with the badly crippled body.

"I woke this morning needing to go to the bathroom. The bell to call the nurses was behind me, pinned to the bed. I can no longer roll over without help. I tried. I tried calling out, but nobody could hear me. I am not soiling my bed if I can help it. The phone was reachable. I dialed 911 and told them to call the nursing home and tell them that the woman in 409 needs to go to the bathroom. Let me tell you, I got quick service."

Way to go, Mom.

Dennis O'Connor, piloting *Stars and Stripes* in the America's Cup, could not beat Ruth going upwind. She always knew when to stop struggling, throw the tiller over, and sneak up to the destination from the other side.

THE UNEXPECTED FLY

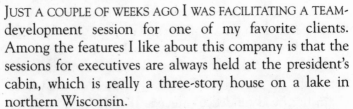

JUST A COUPLE OF WEEKS AGO I WAS FACILITATING A TEAM-development session for one of my favorite clients. Among the features I like about this company is that the sessions for executives are always held at the president's cabin, which is really a three-story house on a lake in northern Wisconsin.

The setting is beautiful. The house is comfortable. The agenda is flexible. Unlike normal conference settings in which I feel some obligation to the general good to set times and pretty much stick to them, in this environment I say that tomorrow we will eat breakfast when most of us have gotten up, and then we will do the following four things, make lunch when we get hungry, and break for recreation when we get done.

Supper is usually at some tiny Wisconsin bar. The boats leave around seven, so from about four to seven everyone recreates in whatever way they choose. Some powerboat around the lake, some take out the motorized water scooters, some hike, some ride all-terrain vehicles, and some sleep. I sit in an outside lounge chair and try to assimilate what I have heard. As an introvert, I need assimilation time.

While I was assimilating, a fly landed on the top of my left thigh. A skinny fly, not too dangerous-looking, perhaps just parking for a moment. Nevertheless I decided to send him to his final reward. I lined him up and swatted a mighty swat. I missed by three inches.

The little devil had jumped diagonally forward. "There

goes another great truth," I muttered to myself. I have always been assured that when escaping, flies jump backward, and I have always assumed that when I missed them, I had not moved fast enough. At fifty-five years old I had finally uncovered from the pile of misinformation poured on me in youth this most salient fact: Some flies jump forward.

I am a better man for this. My kill ratio has increased dramatically. Also, I have once again been reminded that what everyone says has a good chance of being wrong.

How does this happen to us? Does one person see something incorrectly but say it loudly, and everyone else, without thinking, simply repeats it? I don't know how it happens, but here are some truisms that I think deserve correction.

• Work hard and you will get ahead.

I am inclined to doubt this. Working hard does not seem to hurt, but I have seen too many people get ahead without working hard to think it an essential ingredient to success. Talent helps more, verbal skills even more. So do physical characteristics, such as being tall for a man. Have you ever noticed the number of tall vice presidents? It helps a woman not to be too beautiful, but not too ugly either. It helps immeasurably to always please the boss.

People I have known who have gotten ahead have one predominant characteristic and it is not that they have worked hard. It is that they were totally focused on getting ahead and did whatever was necessary.

• Everybody wants to get ahead.

No, they don't. I don't. I wonder if you do. If you did, by now would you not have put this book down and be reading about learning to swim with the sharks? I kept trying halfheartedly to get ahead until one of my friends did me the service of pointing out that I did not really want to do what it took to get on the executive corridor and that I would be uncomfortable playing the game necessary to survive once I did. Since I had always been told that everyone wanted to get ahead, it was hard for me to adapt to the fact that I didn't.

• Work hard now, and get us through these tight times, and the company will remember what you did when we get out of this bind.

I'd like to say this is true because I have been around companies that have been temporarily saved by the free overtime of dedicated employees. When the company finally succeeds, you will be remembered as a hard worker and it will be resented if you back off. You will be remembered by your immediate boss and maybe that person's boss. As soon as those two leave the organization, you will not be remembered at all. There is a good chance that the company will succeed by being bought out and if that happens your odds on being let go are the same as those of the guy loafing alongside you.

I have never seen a company work its way out of trouble. Companies are managed out of trouble. Management is more about thinking than working. If you are in trouble and your management asks you to work harder without offering anything different to do, anything that seems to have a hopeful wisdom to it, float your résumé. This is a sinking ship.

If you are in management, don't ask people to work harder unless you have figured out what is going wrong and how what you are asking them to do will fix it. Bailing vigorously is not helpful in the long run unless the leak has been plugged.

• The company can meet your needs.

The company cannot meet your needs unless your needs are narrowly defined. For instance, friends can be made there, but I, at least, need a broader set of friends than any one company has offered me. I need to be around old people, children, therapists, and ditchdiggers.

The company can no longer meet your needs even for

security. I find that consulting is in some ways safer than being in a company. All my clients will not fire me at once.

There are many axioms out there which we allow to govern our behavior that are not true or not totally true. I encourage you to examine them before trusting your career to them. Maybe they were true at one time and times have changed. Maybe all flies did jump backward at one point in history. But they don't now.

FROM THE HEAD AND THE HEART

HAVE YOU HEARD OF THE MYERS-BRIGGS TYPE INDICATOR? Its categories are: 1) Extrovert, Introvert; 2) Sensing, Intuitive; 3) Thinking, Feeling; and 4) Judging, Perceptive. You need not memorize them. But here in Minnesota it is difficult to survive a cocktail party without a basic understanding of these categories. People walk up to me and say, "Hi, I'm an INTJ."

And I respond, "Oh, is that right? I'm an INTP."

"Thought there was something about you I like. Maybe we could initiate a little dialogue here. That is if your 'P'ness does not get in the way of my 'J'ness." Or maybe I would rather not initiate a dialogue. Maybe I would prefer hiding in the kitchen.

In industry around here I don't think training people teach even basic soldering without inserting a module on the Myers-Briggs types. I like this type-classification system too, and use it frequently. To be more exact, I like it very much, at the same time that I detest it.

I like it because it is nonjudgmental. The categories are a description of eight basic ways of behaving on four variables. Do you get energy from others or from within yourself? Do you prefer the concrete or the abstract? Do you follow your head or your heart? Do you like life tied in neat packages with bow knots, or do you prefer to go with the flow? (This is the short course. The long course takes three days, is much more accurate, and costs more money.)

No matter which way you answer these questions,

there is nothing wrong with you. You are probably a pain in the posterior to people who answer the questions the other way, but you find them annoying too, so all is fair and no complaints. This is the nonjudgmental factor I like so well.

The Myers-Briggs is a great way to start a team-development session. Everyone is affirmed in his or her unique style. I like being able to say, "See how wonderful we all are as people; now let's talk about the difficulties of communicating with one another without blaming one another for being who we are." This is often the start of a friendly, helpful, and boisterous discussion.

That is why I like the Myers-Briggs. Here is why I do not like it.

The person who calls the meeting arrives twenty minutes late. "That's just the way we perceptives are, always late, go with the flow," he says airily. Another person uses being an intuitive as an excuse for getting her facts wrong. The "extrovert" tells me that he need not think deeply on a topic, because extroverts don't do that.

This is sheer nonsense. I am an intuitive. In serious matters I work very hard to be sure that I have my facts straight. I know that this is a problem for intuitives, but knowing that gives me even less of an excuse for failing. I am an introvert, and I put much energy into trying to be a useful group member. I expect extroverts to try to think. It can't be any harder than what I am doing.

But these are petty irritations. The variable that I find personally confusing is the question of following the head or the heart. This is a bind out of which I do not know the way.

People who like to follow their hearts tend to make their decisions not on pragmatic reality but on how they and others will feel about the impact of the decision. They act to maximize the good feeling of themselves and those around them. I don't find many people on an executive level who score as feeling people, but I do find a few.

My client John, regional manager for a computer repair company, used to divide up his sales force's regions based on feeling. This would be called gerrymandering if it were politics. Sam would have five states plus a city in another state so that he would know he was as valued as other regional directors who had six states. Finally the crooked lines on the map would drive John's boss to distraction, so he would insist that John do things rationally, as a thinker would. John then straightened out the lines, and Sam became demotivated. So John would begin working on a special compensation package for Sam. Until John's boss noticed the special compensation packages multiplying and insisted that everyone receive similar treatment. At which point John would add New York City to Sam's western region.

This, however, can be seen as humorous. What I do not understand as a thinking person is why feeling people will not face the facts without getting hurt about it. All I said was that this piece of work was not professionally done. My God, you don't have to cry about it.

Except that I do understand. As often as I declare myself overweight, as soon as someone else declares me overweight, I bleed. My weight is a fact. Why can't I accept it?

A young man I know, when picking up women at the local sports bar, always starts his conversation by telling them that he is interested in bedding them, and if they do not see this as a possibility, he is not interested in buying them a drink. He reports that 90 percent of the women he tries this on tell him he is a jerk and storm off. Ten percent evidence interest and he buys them a drink. He is happy with the results.

I too think he is a jerk. But I must admit I admire his facility at ignoring other people's feelings. I couldn't do it. Of course, the particular game he is playing was never one

I knew how to play, and I doubt that my wife would encourage me to learn it at this phase in our marriage.

However, something like it is useful. Have you ever made cold calls? At one time I was assigned to call every bank in the Twin Cities to solicit interest in our consulting firm's services. It seemed a dumb idea to me, but I was being paid, so I did it. After the third call my feelings about the recipient's feelings died dead. I no longer cared. Somewhat objectively I would say to myself, "This man would like to hang up the phone. I think I will see if I can keep him on another few minutes."

For me this was a freeing experience. I felt like a thinker. In other words, I did not feel. There was no carry-over, however, to the rest of my life. I returned to being deeply disturbed at the idea of upsetting another person. I try to ensure that the waitress remains happy. Sometimes I think this is a sickness.

Much as I admire and dislike the totally pragmatic person, I equally admire and am incapable of imitating the totally feeling person.

One of my friends, a man of some note in his field, explained to me his fee-setting system. First he figures out what he needs to live at his life-style for the year. It is a lordly sum. Then he takes the total number of days in the year, subtracts weekends and holidays, subtracts a month for vacation, subtracts another month for writing, and subtracts a couple more weeks for exercises that do not earn him his full fee. He splits the remaining days in half, and assigns 50 percent to administration and marketing. The remaining 50 percent he divides into the lordly sum. Voilà, his daily rate.

My God, I wish I could do that. "It's what I need," he says. I admire him, and cannot do it. To set my daily rate, I start from what the market will bear for a service such as mine. I work as hard as I can, and if when vacation time rolls around I am on financial target, I take a vacation.

If, in deference to my feelings, I slip down to Pepin for a day of sailing during the week, I spend half the time explaining to myself that this is really all right. I am as likely as not to work the next Saturday to prove that I am not cheating on some imaginary rule that exists somewhere. I can't say I went sailing because I felt like doing it.

If, in deference to the reality I know with my head, I say something or write something that is true but unpleasant, I worry for weeks about all the people I may have offended.

I must say, I am perplexed. I wish I could join one camp or the other, but I cannot. On the shelf to my left sit two books. One is my dream journal. It holds the record of dreams that I have during the night. It is the story of my heart. I take it very seriously. The other book contains my spreadsheet, money earned, bookings, money needed. It is the story of my head. I take that seriously too.

Often they send conflicting messages. What is there to say but "Help!" Maybe this is just the way my life must be lived.

FOOTBALL

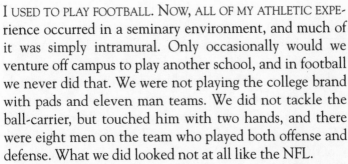

I USED TO PLAY FOOTBALL. NOW, ALL OF MY ATHLETIC EXPE-
rience occurred in a seminary environment, and much of
it was simply intramural. Only occasionally would we
venture off campus to play another school, and in football
we never did that. We were not playing the college brand
with pads and eleven man teams. We did not tackle the
ball-carrier, but touched him with two hands, and there
were eight men on the team who played both offense and
defense. What we did looked not at all like the NFL.

Since I weighed about two hundred fairly solid pounds,
I spent my intramural football career as a lineman. On
offense I blocked the guy across from me. On defense he
and sometimes a couple of others blocked me. Two hundred pounds, before weight-lifting programs and steroids,
was a decent weight. When I played defense, I rated some
attention from the other team. (A highlight of my life is
the time that I attended a religious conference at a college
where the Chicago Bears were holding their training
camp, and two different times the cooks tried to get me to
leave the religious line and get in the Bears' line, where
they thought I belonged.)

For some, our kind of football was racing after passes,
throwing them, gliding around ends, intercepting passes,
breaking up plays. For me, our kind of football was once a
minute having a collision with the guy or guys across from
me. I don't know why I kept doing it. Since it was touch
football, most plays were passing plays. As I fought my

way through obstacles, the opposing quarterback would keep his eye on me, and when I got too close, he would throw the ball. I then returned to the line of scrimmage, and we did it again.

Charlie Hall, weighing forty pounds less than I, is particularly easy to remember. He would get a running start from the backfield of his team. Since I was very slow and he very fast, by the time he reached me he had taken four steps and was flying, and I had taken two and was barely moving. He would throw his body crossways to mine and hit me hard enough to rattle my molars. I was slow but unstoppable. Charlie would drop to the ground, having failed to stop me, and I would grind on into the backfield with the indomitability of a tank and about the same groundspeed. On the next play, we would do it again. Most players did not want to block me. Somehow, I think Charlie liked it a lot. Frustration builds up in a seminary. I helped Charlie relieve his.

After the game I would climb into the shower and notice for the first time the damage he had wrought. I would have bruises from my knees to my rib cage. I would hurt. After a night's sleep it would all stiffen up and I would walk like an old man for the next day. The day after that I would be out there again, getting bruised by someone else, although nobody with Charlie's velocity and bone structure.

And that is what football taught me: how to endure pain—a lesson that has stood me in good stead.

On my shelf there are several books that indicate it is possible to make it through life without pain. One of them tells me that if I but do what I enjoy, the money will follow. Another says that all I lack is a vision, and once I get a clear, bright, specific picture of what I want, it will arrive like magic. This author believes in a world soul that is just waiting to be called upon with my request.

I am doing what I enjoy. I do have a clear vision, and I am working toward it. However, my experience has been that I also suffer a fair amount of pain, pain that can be roughly divided into three categories.

First, a significant portion of my life has been spent being paid for tasks that did not make the best use of my talents. They were tasks I performed fairly well, as well as most people, better than many. But I always felt that I was far from being fully myself while doing them. Therefore I felt some pain. During a two-year period I was doing almost nothing except smoking six cigars a day in my office. That hurt a lot. But I needed the money for my family, and I did not know what else to do. I used to laugh at golden handcuffs, until I found myself wearing them.

I do not regret those years. The books on my shelf said, "You will be better off with no job than with a job that does not satisfy you." It's not that simple. I would not have been better off with no job. I have seen people with no job, and at one time in my life I had about half a job with half an income. It is even less fun than smoking cigars.

I do not advocate simply ignoring this type of pain. I keep those books on my shelf because there is truth in them. A cigar-smoking period is a time for developing a new vision. It is a time to consider what you really enjoy doing. It may be a time to take a salary cut in exchange for a more pleasurable life. But I think rather than jumping too quickly into poverty at the first pinch of a less than perfect work life, one can also view such a period as a time to endure.

The second type of pain is the pain of creation. I have never tried to do something new and better without taking several blows to the chin. Most people do not understand the new idea until it is there in front of them as the completed project. So they shoot at it when it is presented. I too have shot at other people's ideas, ideas that when actualized turned out to be very good indeed, despite my attacks.

An idea never takes on flesh without mistakes. The first time I have tried anything it has always bombed. Then comes all the advice from the cheap seats, some of it good, some of it bad, but most of it loaded with the insinuation that if the advice giver had been the one running this project, these problems would not have occurred. Like heck they wouldn't have.

Finally the thing is done. The project is in place. But never without pain.

The third type of pain is the general anxiety of living. All the world religions have pointed out that if you are going to have anything, along with what you have will come the fear of losing it. That has checked out with my experience. For that very reason, I do not seek to have riches by Donald Trump's standards.

But I have not chosen, as the world religions advise, to live detached from worldly goods. I live well above the poverty line. I have a good house, two cars, a lovely boat, and the aspiration of paying my children's college tuition. I even hope for some financial comfort in my old age. I have been asked how I can keep myself motivated to work when I work alone, often in my home office. Why don't I grab a beer from the refrigerator and turn on the TV? Because every morning I wake up with a gnawing feeling beneath my breastbone that none of my clients will call, that my in-company courses are not going to fill, and that my editor is going to reject the chapters I mailed in last week. This particular pain I hope never goes away. I need it in order to get out of bed. I am pleased with the projects it forces me to undertake.

So I thank Charlie Hall and all those other blockers who raised welts on my flesh. They taught me that pain can be endured—a valuable lesson for life. Maybe the authors who say that there is some easy way to slide through without suffering know something I don't. My experience has been that there is a price tag on everything, even on being alive. And the price tag reads, "It hurts."

DROUGHT

THIS YEAR IT IS RAINING. I DO NOT KNOW IF IT IS THE wettest year on record, but it is the wettest year that I remember. My wife left for two weeks at the start of July, giving me explicit instructions to water her flowers. I have never had to. We have had a solid rain every other day for the two weeks.

The three years before this, we had a drought. At first I barely noticed. I had a spring of unusually fine sailing weather—one bright day after another, not a lot of wind, but enough. It was the year that the fungi on Lake Pepin formed in July instead of August and grew so thick that when I would hit a heavy patch, the smell was similar to that of a freshly mowed lawn.

By the next year everyone was talking about the lack of rain. My backyard lawn, which had a southern exposure, was brown and not responding to the sprinkler. The third year, the drought began to get to me. I turned on the cable weather channel four times a day to stare at the radar picture, hoping to see rain on the screen.

This year the drought has broken. Rain and more rain pours on the ground. The wet ground heated by the sun produces storm after storm. The cycle of wetness has returned. Now I count the drought's blessings.

I notice that the woods have thinned out. The weaker trees could not take it. They have died and are being toppled a few at a time by rot and this year's winds. New vegetation is taking their place, greener, stronger, younger. Room has been made for new growth.

We are in a drought in American industry. The rain of foreign dollars in search of our goods and services has slowed. Some of our towering giant corporations are feeling the effects, shriveling in the absence of the green rain. Only the strongest of our growth corporations continue to expand, and even they do so fitfully, extending branches and roots first one way and then another, searching for a vein of groundwater or a passing shower. "Niche marketing" is shorthand for recognizing that it is getting dry out there. It is best to find small pockets of water.

Many of us endure our personal droughts, cast out by the organizations that lack the cash to keep even useful people in useful jobs. Because my role takes me from place to place, I frequently have referred to me people searching for a job, people who hope I may be able in turn to refer them to one of the guardians of the successful springs in town. Without wanting to, I am beginning to understand some things about this drought.

I would not want to be in a big corporation. I teach leadership in one of them. There is something about the big corporation that attracts or creates dependent people. I am supposed to be getting the cream of their crop, and I find that very few of the participants in my classes possess the ability to succeed in tough times. They do not know how to search on their own for new sources of income. They depend on the corporation finding it for them. They do not know how to skinny an operation down so that it can survive on minimal income. Their versions of skinny a small corporation would call fat.

These are not bad people. They are so insulated from the outside world that they do not experience the drought until it gets them. They are inside the house with the air-conditioning on and everything working as usual. One day the tap runs dry, and it is too late to do anything about it. From where they sit inside the large corporate house, there was little they could have done about it anyway.

I do not know if the big corporations will collapse. That is hard to imagine. But each day they feel more like dry husks to me. I have more hope for the smaller corporations. One of my clients has a bell in the center of the second floor. When a major new order is signed, the line manager of the signing unit rings the bell and everyone in the building can come and hear the salesperson explain what the new order is, how it was obtained, and what it will mean for the corporation. Everybody in that company knows whether it is raining or not. Everybody is trying to respond to the situation.

As corporations large and small attempt to downsize, people tossed out need not take it personally. One of my recent visitors had spent the last five years pulling together the sloppy computer operations of a major health company. When it came time for them to lighten ship, they noticed that his operation was running smoothly and no longer needed him, and that is how his life raft appeared on my beach.

The personal drought can be very useful, if the person experiencing it does not panic. It is a good time to meet your own family. It is a time for others to understand what the producer has been producing. It is a time for others to pitch in and help. It is a time to wander around and see what has been going on in other industries. It is a time to reassess what you really want out of life and see if you can find it.

This requires some faith that all droughts come to an end. So far that seems to be the way nature works. On the far side of the drought a person can live a richer life, be in a more satisfying place, have roots in soil that suits one's skills, and often be financially in a better place.

I do think I smell it. There is rain in the air. A cooling blanket is being drawn down on American industry and it is finding more companies pruned and ready to take advantage of the financial rain, ready to produce the quality products and services that will keep the cycle going.

I do not think it will ever be as wet as it was in the years after the Second World War. There are too many other parched fields across the globe willing to do anything for water. But then I have never wanted to live in a rain forest; that is much too lush for me.

It is all right by me if we have a little dryness to keep us conserving our water and pulling our weeds, but come on, Mother Nature, and the global economic forces, let the rains come again. We are nearly ready.

SMOOTH SAILING

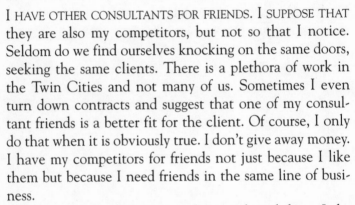

I HAVE OTHER CONSULTANTS FOR FRIENDS. I SUPPOSE THAT they are also my competitors, but not so that I notice. Seldom do we find ourselves knocking on the same doors, seeking the same clients. There is a plethora of work in the Twin Cities and not many of us. Sometimes I even turn down contracts and suggest that one of my consultant friends is a better fit for the client. Of course, I only do that when it is obviously true. I don't give away money. I have my competitors for friends not just because I like them but because I need friends in the same line of business.

A couple of weeks ago I took a gentle sail down Lake Pepin. Pepin is not the size of Lake Superior, and certainly not the size of the Atlantic, but when the boat is only twenty-three feet long, a twenty-five-mile-long lake, running between two and three miles wide, will do nicely. I went west, with a following breeze, and had covered about eight miles when the wind picked up in intensity behind me. It was time to turn back anyway, so I flipped the *Laughing Buddha* around. Quickly the wind lifted from about fifteen knots to about thirty-five, and the waves began to build.

I doused the working jib. The *Buddha* sails well in winds between twenty-five and forty-five knots on the mainsail alone. I began tacking my way back against waves that had risen to about three feet, whitecaps and the works. Since the *Buddha* is short, she pitches a fair amount in any waves, so I snuggled into a life vest, not so much out of fear of hitting the water as out of fear of breaking a rib as I moved about the cockpit and cabin.

In these conditions sailing turns into work. My biceps feel the strain of the tiller. Making a sandwich is impossible, and lighting a pipe becomes a major operation. I set the autohelm and bounced my way below deck. Jammed the pipe full of tobacco. I tried to get the pipe and the match to connect amidst the jarring, then bounced my way back to the autohelm. I released it and corrected course for the wind variation that waited to occur until I was out of reach of the tiller. By that time the pipe had gone out.

After the first hour the wind dropped to about twenty-five knots. This is the borderline between being comfortable with the jib up or needing to have it as I had it, down. The *Buddha* was moving too slowly for my patience, so I put the jib back in place.

Oh, yes indeed, I did begin to move. I even wondered about the wisdom of my decision and thought about lowering the jib again. I left my comfortable seat and stood up so I could see the wind coming at me over the water and position the boat to dump the excess air before I lay too much on my side. Now I was banging through the waves at a ferocious clip. Spray was coming back into the cockpit. I was not wearing anything waterproof and was getting uncomfortably wet.

While in this condition I passed two of my acquaintances from the dock. I passed them because they were not headed as close into the wind as I was. "Now that's a good idea," I thought. "If I were to be as clever as they, I'd drop this baby off ten degrees and not be quite so miserable. Aw, heck, I'll just keep on and get myself off the lake where I can get dry."

As I swung by the other boat, I took my hand off of the

lifeline for a brief moment, shouted, and waved. He waved back and we plowed on, he on the gentler course, I hurrying to get off the lake.

"Man," I thought. "Now there is one smart dude. That guy knows how to sail a boat. He is having fun out here and all I can think of is putting this boat in the slip.

He came in about an hour after I did. I helped him tie up. "I couldn't hear what you were shouting at me out there," he said.

"I was saying that we have too much wind."

"Oh, yeah, maybe so, but your boat sure sails into the wind well," he said. "I can't get mine nearly as close. And you make it look so easy, standing at the tiller like that, waving at people you are passing."

That is the reason I like having friends in the same business as I am. It always seems to me that I am struggling and everybody else just floats through work with everything going their way. I feel so incompetent at responding to the demands of business.

Then I sit down with my friends and we chat. I find out that they are having trouble finding clients. I find out that they are not sure if what they are doing is adding one whit to the good of the universe. I find out that they want my advice, as I want theirs, for we have precisely the same problems, doubts, and fears. I no longer feel alone.

A suggestion I made to a client whose organization was severely troubled was that he call all thirty of his employees into a room, provide coffee and donuts, and let everybody talk for half a day about what they were feeling. There would be no need to do anything about it, just officially acknowledge that their current plight is not much fun, and let everybody say their piece. He could not see what that would accomplish, so he did not take the suggestion. What it would have accomplished is that everyone would know it was the situation that was the problem, not them. And they would know that they were not alone.

I regularly attend the meetings of the local branch of my professional society. I do it because I need to belong to something. But I do not enjoy attending. The meetings resemble a five-year high-school reunion. Everybody is trying to impress everybody else. They all have the biggest clients or the best jobs, with the highest incomes and the most spectacular techniques. I leave the meeting feeling next to worthless and somewhat uncomfortable about the white lies I have told.

I need friends who confide their humanity to me to let me know that I am doing all right.

I think I may walk down the dock one of these days and tell my fellow sailor how impressed I am with the way he handles a boat, how much I admire his willingness to cope with weather. I might even tell him how embarrassed I am at my concerns about getting a little wet or bounced around. He did me the favor of an honest compliment. I owe him one back.

I have a hunch that a little disclosure from me on this might turn him from an acquaintance to a friend.

FAT BOY

NOW THAT I AM A SHADE BEYOND FIFTY-FIVE YEARS OLD, I am returning to a physical condition I have not been in since grade school. In high school I became interested in sports. I played almost every sport playable. Some I played well, and some just enthusiastically. I have continued to do so throughout most of my life. So while I have always tended toward the heavy end of the spectrum, most of the time it was a lineman's heaviness—some fat, lots of muscle. I don't think others saw me as out of shape, just heavy.

That is changing. Although my weight is holding constant, it's all softening. I feel folds of soft fat. I puff on the stairs. I avoid bending. I prefer sitting in chairs to taking a walk. I am falling apart. I am reminded of my childhood.

During my grade school years I was a fat boy.

The daily paper recently cited a study in which children were offered their choice of friends from a series of pictures. The pictures were of children from a variety of races and with different handicaps. The children ordered by rank those who they might pick as a friend. It did not surprise me to find out that the fat kid was always ranked last. I have been there.

Our family moved several times during the grade-school years, so I became quite used to being new to the playground pecking order, standing on the side, waiting to be invited in. I do not want to mislead you. Frequently I was invited in, I always made a few friends, and my childhood was not one great black cloud of fatness. But my weight was an always-present fact.

I do not know if this happens to people who are not fat, but at every playground I moved to, my arrival always provoked a fight. Somebody or several people would come over to me, but one would pick the fight. A couple of references to my bulgy body, a couple of shoves, and then my dignity could take it no longer and the war was on.

I learned several things from this. I learned that in order to prevent more fights I did not need to win this one. All I needed to do was make the other guy so miserable he and his buddies never wanted to do this again. I lost more fights than I won. Winning was always a bit of a surprise. I never knew what to do with it, except quit. Losing I understood. When losing I never stopped fighting until some teacher pried my antagonist and me apart. Even when he won, he never did it again. If nothing else, fighting me was a tedious experience.

Some ideas that I gained from this experience are stored in my mental file under the heading "Fat-Boy Psychology."

First, there are many ways of being a fat boy. One of them is to be an ugly girl. Another is to be dumb. Another is to be unlovable. And of course, there is too short, or too tall, or too skinny, or even too smart. Each of these differences from the norm can exile a child to the edge of the playground.

Second, the bearer never forgets the label, no matter how hard he or she struggles to leave it behind. I have a friend who on turning fifty became simply good-looking. When I first met her in her thirties, she was stunning. Now I can talk with her calmly; then I had to remember to keep breathing normally. Sometimes I would forget to breathe at all. She had been an "ugly girl." In her middle teens she decided to improve on nature and worked on her way of holding herself, her clothes, her cosmetics. At the same time, Mother Nature decided to give the ugly duckling a break and turned her into a swan. Ma Nature and she were a potent combination with a breathtaking result. She still thought of herself as a less-than-attractive woman. She still struggled to look beautiful. She had difficulty understanding other people's reactions, did not know that she filled men with desire and women with envy. These grade-school labels stick.

I know executives who put their every degree or certificate on their walls in an effort to get beyond being the "dumb kid." The short man with Napoleonic needs is a stereotype that holds a kernel of truth. The tall woman, who could be a grand vision of strength, slouches across her office to take my hand, her shoulders pulled together and held low to disguise the fact that she is taller than I; she is still hoping she will be invited to the prom. The sensitive person listens closely for the words that will tell that I too find him or her unloveable. The salesman conceals his erudition behind a stream of obscenities and slang.

Many of us got racked up back in those early years. We do things to get over it. We get degrees, lift weights, buy cosmetics, hire therapists, but I don't know that anyone ever completely undoes that damage. It's too bad.

If you are one of us fat boys, I want you to realize that you are not alone. I want you to read in a business book that there are many of us out here doing our best to be our best and contribute our best who expect any moment that the audience is going to snigger at us, put us down, hit us with sarcasm, point out that we do not belong. No, it won't happen, at least it hasn't happened to me yet, but still, deep down, the fear persists. So we struggle with it and always will, for what else is there to do?

If you have been spared this particular experience, I would like you to know that many have not. It may help you understand why the woman you envy for her looks continues to overdress for the office. It may help you to understand the man who runs five miles every lunch hour. It may help you to understand the person who insists on listing his master's degree on his business card. It may help you understand the obnoxious guy who invites you to prove that you dislike him.

I was running an in-company interpersonal-skills training workshop that required working in teams. I decided not to assign people but to have them stand in the middle of the room and select their own week's companions, without using words, just pointing and walking and tugging. All of the beautiful and charming people in the room selected one another and became one group. So immediate was their decision that they sealed other people out by closing their circle, turning their backs, and joining their hands. I was furious. That was not at all what I had had in mind. I had hoped that they would give others the benefit of their interpersonal skills.

Workshop participants had taken an inventory that evaluated them on, among other things, their sense of self-worth. While scoring these evaluations I found that all of the beautiful people had a poor sense of their own self-worth. I ran a course in interpersonal skills for everybody else. This group ran its own therapy sessions through every day and well into every night.

Now there is a phenomenon a fat boy can understand.

ON LEADERSHIP

A COUPLE OF YEARS AFTER MY ORDINATION, I WAS INCHING my Volkswagen Bug down a suburban parkway, traffic half blocked by the barricades and blue trucks of Minnegasco. I remembered the Friday they told me I was going to work for Olson. At eighteen, I was already a veteran summer-vacation fill-in on service crews (my dad was the union president). I knew something was up when the superintendent visiting my foreman continually glanced my way. It was left to the foreman to give me the news. He was hesitant and awkward. "I'm sorry," he said. "Next Monday you will have to report to work with Olson." He never said why he was sorry. "Oh, he's a nice guy, but you'll find out for yourself."

On Monday I showed up for work. I was ten minutes early, and scared. I noticed that, unlike any other crew I had worked on, everyone else was there, sitting in their cars. Two minutes before start time a short and stocky blonde-haired man climbed out of his car and headed for the toolbox trailer, and on that signal everyone else promptly joined him. I went too.

"You're Cowan? I'm Olson. We're done here. Moving. Here's the new address. Guys will introduce themselves. Follow the ditcher if you don't know the way. I'm going now." As we tossed the barricades onto the trailer and hooked the trailer to the ditcher, the guys did introduce themselves, five men with the same conspiratorial grin.

The next address was in Dinkytown, an old hotel next to the Campus Theater. It was there I found out what this mysterious job was about. Olson stood next to a pile of industrial pipe three times the diameter of anything I had ever handled. "You guys, go see what you think. Cowan, go with 'em."

We descended the back stairs, worked our way through a crawlspace to the front wall, then back out to the street, swinging the metal finder to locate the main. Then they reported in. "Gotta hand-carry the bleeping pipe into the bleeping basement, no way to get a crane on it."

"Gotta weld the bleeping pipe down in that crawl hole; one bleeping mistake and the bleeping hotel burns up."

"Can't use the bleeping ditcher, gotta hand tunnel out from the bleeping basement."

"That's what I thought," said Olson with satisfaction. And all five of them were smiling back at him as if they had been granted a month's vacation. "So let's do it."

And we did it. With speed and joy and precision. After two days of constant sweat the only sign of our presence was six inches of capped pipe sticking into the basement and a square of fresh asphalt in the street.

"Moving," said Olson. "Brooklyn Center, here's the address, Greenhouse, set way back, don't know way follow ditcher, I'm going ahead, you hook up." And this time I was grinning too.

It was a simple conspiracy. We were the small main and industrial crew. If it was tough to do, and it had to be done by hand, it was assigned to us. And we could do what nobody else could do, or at least that is what Olson had us convinced was true.

At the Greenhouse I learned one more thing about Olson. We were nearly done, all the pipe hooked and laid, valves in place and air-tested. I grabbed a shovel and started to backfill ("Can't use bleeping backhoe. Ruin bleeping lawn."). The senior laborer stopped me. "Gotta wait for bleeping engineers." It seemed that sometime before, they used to give Olson engineering drawings on how to do these complex jobs. Then he had to correct the drawings and tell the engineers how the job should be done. In a dramatic burst of uncommon organizational good sense, the engineers now let Olson put in the job, then they came out and drew it the way he had done it. After a pair of men in dress suits had respectfully walked their way through the job, the word was passed—"Fill 'er"—and so the summer sped by.

What made Olson a leader?

1. He was always a step or three ahead of the game. Unlike other crews, we never waited for stuff; it was there.
2. He had a vision of what he wanted and he shared it and held us to it.
3. His values showed in every bead of sweat he generated.
4. We decided what to do; he corrected seldom, only when needed.
5. He understood himself better than most people do. "Don't know if I should take it," he told me when he was offered a promotion to superintendent. "Like using my hands too much."

It's Richard E. Byrd's theory of leadership I have used in analyzing Olson, but with all due respect to behavioral science, if the theory and Olson had not matched, I'd question the theory. I know a leader when I have followed one.

Which brings me back to the time ten years later that I was inching along in my VW. I had never worked on a main crew, and so why was this main crew provoking familiar feelings? Watching them grind merrily down the street, hearing the cheerful obscenities through the window, observing them move at a near trot from task to task. The answer came at the head of the line. Two men were cutting asphalt on the lead jackhammers. One was young, tanned, stripped to the waist. The other was older, wearing dress pants, a white shirt, and a tie. All these clothes were in the process of ruin. I parked my car, snuck down the sidewalk, and tapped the tie wearer on the shoulder. He peered at me through his protective goggles, trying to recognize the face above the clerical suit and roman collar.

"Olson, you're a superintendent," I said. "Get your bleeping hands off the bleeping equipment before the bleeping union has your bleeping bleep."

"Oh, Cowan," his face lighted up. "Things were slowing down up here. Thought I'd give 'em a hand. Got other things to do. This stuff is tough to cut. Worst I ever saw. You want to take it for a while?"

I nearly did.

NAMING GOD

IN BUSINESS WE DO NOT TALK ABOUT GOD. IN CHURCH WE do not talk about business. I am not sure that this is the best way to function.

In a Lakota village a century ago, if you wanted to know the religious thoughts and aspirations of the people, you needed only to look at the pictures and symbols painted on the outer wall of the teepee. Workers, warriors, hunters, and fishermen recorded their religious dreams there. Indeed, the person's name was the product of a religious experience. The morning libations, the preparation for the hunt, the moment of kill, and the coming of the seasons were all times of prayer, times of acknowledging a force greater than that of the individual or even the tribe. Business decisions, such as moving the village, seeking new places to hunt, or attacking a competitor, were not made on a rational basis alone. Councils were prayer meetings.

In business we Euro-Americans think that as lovely and pastoral as that picture is, nothing similar to it is in our history. We have short memories. The business culture of the United States was founded by Puritans and their fellow travelers. They did discuss God at the office, and they did discuss business in church. One reason that they were so willing to develop and embrace a market-place without government control, a marketplace where each individual could operate freely without confining legal boundaries, was that they themselves were thoroughly controlled by the common morality and tenets of a deeply held and persistently reinforced religion.

When they visualized economic and business freedom, they visualized the freedom of men already held under restraint. They would have been horrified at leveraged buyouts. "What has this man added to creation?" they would have asked. "What good has he done?" They could not imagine a man so free from religious restraint that he would seek benefit without contribution. When such men were found, they were held without honor, rejected from the community of the church and the community of other businessmen. Such people were certainly not to be regarded as worthy of praise simply because their dealings created personal wealth.

Businessmen of that day were not businessmen from expediency, they were businessmen by vocation. As the preacher had been called to preach, the teacher called to teach, they were called by God to develop and run a business. They approached their task with the intensity of purpose and the rigid ethics of a celibate monk. Quite successfully too.

A century later my grandfather took the train from northern Minnesota to Fargo, North Dakota—no small journey in those days—to discuss a business deal. The man he met over dinner laid out a persuasive case for the profitable connection of my grandfather's money (he was a banker) and his own oil-drilling project. Before retiring, they agreed to meet for breakfast at eight in the morning to seal the deal. Grandfather was leaving on the 9:30 train. My grandfather was at the table at eight. At nine a flustered hotel clerk brought a note from the other man saying that he had overslept and inquiring whether Grandfather would take a later train. He returned the note, writing on the back, "I do not work with people who can't keep appointments." He got on the train.

Ferocious, oh, my, yes. I am not recommending similar ferocity. I am pointing out that at one time there was a commonly held value system about which there was no question. When Grandfather returned to International Falls and was asked by friends how the deal went, he would respond, "He was an hour late for the appointment." Everyone knew that that meant no deal. A man who was not punctual violated the value system and was not trusted to be honest, cost-conscious, or shrewd.

In the early thirties, Grandfather's bank failed. It was not his fault. It was a time when many banks failed. In his day there were bankruptcy laws, as there are now. His personal wealth—and he was wealthy—was safe. Except he did not use the bankruptcy laws. In his eyes he had failed the trust placed in him by God. Banking was not his job, it was his vocation. He had held and loaned other people's money in a sacred trust. In expiation for his failure in vocation, he folded his personal wealth into the bank's assets and allowed it to be spread out among the bank's creditors.

Ferocious, oh, my, yes. I don't recommend this either. Each creditor gained a nickel, and my father moved to the cities to work in a parking lot and support his widowed mother, the old man having compounded the tragedy by dying. But it does speak to the value system firmly in place in that business community that Grandfather was regarded neither as a hero nor a dolt. In their eyes he had done what a man should. He was a baptized Christian, wasn't he? The knot of Irish Roman Catholics, that tightly bound community struggling to wrench a living from the rocky soil of northern Minnesota, knew what God wanted of a man in his position. My great-uncle who was chairman of the board chose to use the bankruptcy laws for his own protection. He immediately moved out of the community. There was no other choice. He would never have been trusted or accepted again.

The Puritans and the Roman Catholics of northern Minnesota were able to create a common value system because they knew the name of God. Each in their own era and place belonged to a community that was certain that there was a power behind the universe and that they could define the nature of that power and its demands on them. They knew the name of God.

We are no longer so sure. We have intermingled our nationalities, races, and beliefs. When we value the person in the next office and know that his belief, his picture, his name for God is different from ours, we are no longer confident in what we were taught. If we remain confident that what we were taught is correct, we are at least silent about it in respect to his or her right to religious peace in the office setting. We have undertaken a conspiracy of silence about God.

This is counterproductive. It cuts us off from the deeper aspects of our humanity. To listen to fifteen executives discuss a business decision in the boardroom is to listen to fifteen people who do not believe in God. Except that privately they do. Some are passionate members of a fundamentalist, evangelical church. There are a couple of Roman Catholics, a Lutheran, and a Jew. If it is a boardroom, there is at least one Episcopalian, probably the senior warden at his church. The range of religions is represented, as is the range of intensity of belief, from tepid to passionate. Perhaps there is one atheist, who when asked will say, "Well, of course, I believe in some power greater than us, but I don't believe in God." My favorite atheist has more deeply held religious values pressed on him by his "greater power" than I do.

The Puritans and the Catholics of northern Minnesota each had a name for God held commonly in each of their communities. We do not have a common name for God.

Theologically we are more correct than they were. No one has an accurate picture of God. The medieval theologian Thomas Aquinas wrote a summary of theology in the very beginning of which he sets out to define God. He begins by saying that the task cannot be done. If God is God, God is more than us, and the lesser cannot hold the more. Naming God is similar to pouring a quart of water into a pint jar. One leaves out quite a bit. I do not know if I have seen an invalid description of God. I have seen partial descriptions, each having some ring of truth, and all slightly smelling of manure. Thomas would have said that if I piled all those partial descriptions together, I would still have only a partial description. The unnameable cannot be named.

Thomas was a mystic. He had personally felt the presence of God. On his deathbed, he asked that his writings be destroyed. He felt that despite the acclaim others gave him, basically he had missed the boat. The unnameable cannot be named.

It is precisely in recognizing this fact that conversations about God in business can occur. The Lakota were here before us. When the Christian missionaries told them about Jesus of Nazareth, many Lakota sought immediate baptism. They were moved by this story until they discovered that the missionaries expected them to give up their original beliefs. These original beliefs did not exclude the possibility that in other places and other times other people had arrived at worthwhile beliefs and practices. They could incorporate the story of Jesus into their system. They found, however, that the missionaries did not share their open-systems attitude. The missionaries had named God. The Lakota had not.

I have seen some attempts at introducing God into business. I am not comfortable with them. The New Age movement provides business courses that they say are not sectarian or even theological, but rather about a new brand of psychology. My practiced ear hears them naming God quite definitively. I do not wish God to enter business through their doorway.

Some corporations allow the Christians to gather for

prayer breakfasts under the company's roof. Although such breakfasts tend more to the fundamentalist and evangelical end of the spectrum than my own position, I do not personally mind them. I even attend from time to time, lustily singing the hymns, wincing only slightly at the theology, and deeply enjoying the fact that we can admit we have beliefs and pray together in the same setting in which we work. I felt good about these events until I discussed them with a friend of mine who said he never felt so thoroughly Jewish as when the Christians were singing hymns in the cafeteria. He found himself wondering when the pogrom would start. I do not think he is completely paranoid. I do not wish God to enter business through this door either.

My vision is this. If we can all admit that our name for God is incomplete, then, like the Lakota, we can gain from one another's experience of God without violating our own. I see a business world in which we know one another as religious beings. We know one another's religious backgrounds, churches, and present beliefs. I see a business world in which major decisions are made based not only on economic facts. I see decision makers inquiring of one another what each person's god would want, what each person's religious heritage would say, what each person discovered the night before while communing with God, or the Talking-God, or the collective unconscious, or that something that is greater than all of us.

If you find this frightening, remember that most generations of the human race made their decisions precisely in this manner. We are the anomaly.

Now, that I find frightening.

ON HOLDING
BACK THE DARK

I DO NOT HAVE MANY CHANCES TO TALK ABOUT Christmas. I have been a priest for twenty-eight years and have preached at the midnight service only twice. Now I always take the family service at five o'clock on Christmas Eve. My sermon is a story for the little kids, one I almost make up as I go along, with God thundering from the clouds and eight-foot angels appearing to several small children who by some coincidence have the same names as the children from the congregation. It is great fun, but not exactly theology.

I am not complaining. I think it is the pastor's prerogative, even duty, to speak to the community in the middle of Christmas Eve night. When it is cold and dark, the flock should hear from the shepherd, not from me.

But that leaves me with twenty-six years of Christmas thought with no account in which to deposit it, except perhaps this one. And that is what I am going to do. I am going to say something about Christmas right here, briefly, so if you don't want to read it, now is almost the time to stop.

Christmas is all about the dark. And being afraid of it. And admitting it. And only then looking for the light, which shines ever so much more brightly on those who know they are afraid of the dark. Now is the time to stop, if you don't want to read some theology.

I used to resent the pagan incursion into the Christmas season, the crass commercialism of the make-a-buck community forcing the door to my pious little stable, butting into the love story of mother and child, interrupting the angel chorus. Then I relooked at my history and realized that the pagans were here first. It was their feast, and we Christians decided to horn in on the action, subvert their story, and impose our own.

And what was their story? They were afraid of the dark! It grew cold, and the fires were lit longer. Every year they huddled by the blaze, wondering if full days would ever come again, or if these days—with the fade of the sun, the chill of the earth, blackness—were the last, the end.

Then the sun began its return. They celebrated the end of a terribly unscientific fear, but one that plagued them deeply, burrowing into their confidence about life. They celebrated by lighting bonfires, as we light candles. They danced in the forests, as we exchange gifts. They told stories of the gods, and we tell the story of Jesus.

I like our answer to the fear better than I like theirs. But they have one gift that we do not have, and that is a straightforward look at the fear itself. This fear of the dark, this foreshadowing of the grave, this anticipation of death crept over them during this cold month. No touching a switch on the wall to bathe them in light. No adjusting a thermostat to banish the cold. No reference to scientific texts as reassurance of an annual cycle soon to be over. They had to face the fear of death yearly. It is a gift.

Fear driven into the corner is still fear. We are no less afraid than they were. We use our technology and our scientific understanding, our hyperactive life-styles and our pathetic consumerism, every ounce of our energy to drive to the farthest corners of consciousness the fact that there is an unavoidable darkness waiting for us. How much of our grim seriousness about success—at work, family, even at play—is an attempt to avoid the fact that all lives end, and therefore all lives by definition end in failure? We say, "His heart failed" or "Her kidneys failed" in a hurt tone of voice, as if that was not precisely what they were designed to do sometime. And if we concentrate really hard and are successful in all we do, perhaps then our kidneys and our heart will never fail, and then there will be no dark. Or at least if we focus on other things, we need never see the dark, except that one time when it surprises us.

Without darkness there is no light. The candlelit creche in church is beautiful because of the darkness without. The spring flower is welcome compared to the frozen white. Friends are glorious because they will not always be there. A baby's skin demands touch because soon it will hang loosely on an old woman's weakening hand. A good work is satisfying because it will be left behind. Any breath is precious because it is nearly the last.

If we are unwilling to be aware of the dark, we cannot see the light.

My Christmas suggestion to myself, and to you if you are willing to hear it, is to turn off from time to time the incandescent bulb of this most commercial season and grow comfortable with the dark. Understand mortality, try to accept it, for this dark doorway leads into the gloriously lit playroom called life.

WHO WILL SING OUR SONG?

THIS LINE OF THINKING WAS PAINFULLY ETCHED IN MY heart as I attended Sheldon Tart's funeral. The priest spoke eloquently about Sheldon's role in the community and his place in his family. Rudy Boschwitz spoke simply and even tenderly about Sheldon and the Republican party. But there was only the slightest mention of what he had meant to the corporation.

It was in the corporation that he had spent most of his time. If he devoted more energy to anything else, he was indeed a miracle worker, for in the corporation he worked most people off their feet. He was dearly loved by those with whom he worked. His genius was the single most important cause for the existence of one entire successful division. Half of the people at the funeral were from the corporation. We said nothing.

There was no avenue for saying anything. Two half columns announcing his death in the company newsletter was all I ever saw, and yet I know many who experienced deep private grief that deserved corporate expression.

I must explain what I mean as I use words such as *corporate* and *company*. When I was a young boy, we used to sing this campfire song: "Oh come all you fellows and join in a song—long live the company." I can imagine the voyagers who first sang it gathered around their campfire, rejoicing in the difficult miles they had put behind them and in the fellowship, the company, that together had done it. When I use the word *company*, it is that fellowship I see. The company is not the charter papers, not the stockholders nor the executives, but all of its members together.

During my all-too-brief stint as a corporate manager, I had this insane desire to keep a bottle of scotch in my desk, because at the end of the workday I wanted to take fifteen minutes to drink with my coworkers. I did not want the elaborate mess of journeying to a bar. I wanted fifteen minutes of intellectual numbness and emotional fullness to celebrate the end of today's whirlwind with my friends and coworkers, the company.

It is not that corporations don't do something. I was kidding the receptionist at the Cray software facility for not putting my name on the welcome board. She said you had to buy a Cray computer to get that honor. Not true! The next day the welcome board congratulated an employee on the birth of her baby. Elaine Millam tells me of Honeywell Residential's huge parties at the close of successful cycles. Doug Baker tells me of the beer and popcorn get-togethers IDS has initiated. I remember the annual trip to the Excelsior amusement park with my dad to enjoy another year of success with Minnegasco. No, we do do something.

So why do I remain troubled? Good things are happening. What's missing?

We ended a team-development session a couple of weeks ago on a note of pleasant success. We were done. We knew it. There was a moment of satisfied silence. Don Johnson, my coconsultant, leaned toward me with some seriousness and a hint of kidding and said, "Give us a benediction, Father." I looked around and saw that others were ready for something. I reached down inside for the words, and nothing came. It was a solemn moment and I blew it.

First of all, as I said to them, "I do not know whose name to invoke." As I sit here, I still do not know. I have too much respect for whatever their beliefs are to have used some formula that arises from my belief and is offensive to them. The name to be invoked was the name of the company, and as a consultant, an outsider, I had no right to invoke it.

Secondly, I was afraid to be solemn in the business environment, where I have never seen solemnity. Promotion parties are usually laced with put-down humor about the promotee. Achievement awards are usually awkwardly given. Twenty years of service to the company is celebrated with two minutes and a pen at the end of a staff meeting. The sugary cake of going away parties leaves me hungry for something more. The luncheon at Chi-Chi's restaurant is a fragmented and awkward expression of a solid and living bond forged while working together. Others may have seen better, but this has been my experience.

I did take the risk once, with no regrets. When Betty Martin left Control Data, we held a party at Mayslack's bar. I gathered the gang in the parking lot afterward and read the passage from Proverbs describing the valiant woman. For me it was a grave and serious moment. I ignored my fears about what everyone else might feel and gave it my evangelical best, for Betty is a valiant woman and deserved to be told so. The passage ends, "Give her credit for all she does. She deserves the respect of everyone." I still wonder what the gossip was on that one! But Betty liked it.

One of the Christian mystics claimed that he never saw a human being without seeing two seraphim with flaming candles escorting that person. When our lives are lived in service to the organization, should not the organization provide for the solemn moments?

My suggestion is a book of ceremonies, expressing the company feelings at times of passage. Among the ceremonies included would be: the reception of a new employee into the company; the installation of a manager; the appointment of an executive; the celebration of years of service; the mourning of the death of a coworker; and the celebration of successful accomplishments.

Each ceremony would begin and end with words to be read aloud that have been crafted to express feeling dramatically. Each ceremony would have room for informal statements from individuals. Some of these ceremonies would express the trust and responsibility the corporation is placing in the person. Each ceremony would express the corporation's gratitude for the gift of time from a human life, the one thing that once given can never be taken back.

I know this can be done. I am certain that we deserve it to be done. Our accomplishments are not too simple, mundane, and ordinary to merit a moment of glory. We deserve to have our fellow workers sing our song. We owe them a poem in their honor.

FOR THE CHILDREN

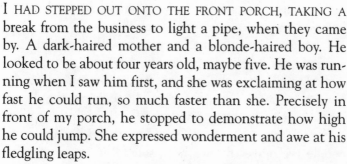

I HAD STEPPED OUT ONTO THE FRONT PORCH, TAKING A break from the business to light a pipe, when they came by. A dark-haired mother and a blonde-haired boy. He looked to be about four years old, maybe five. He was running when I saw him first, and she was exclaiming at how fast he could run, so much faster than she. Precisely in front of my porch, he stopped to demonstrate how high he could jump. She expressed wonderment and awe at his fledgling leaps.

I am sad for the children. Soon this time will pass. Soon she will send him off to school. At first there will be only a little difference. Then the screws will be tightened, the lathe turned on, and he will be formed and bent to live in the world that you and I live in.

There is a southern Minnesota poet of some fame who allows that he became a poet because the small town in which he lived was dominated by old-country people, as was the small school. They shared his poetry with one another, praised his genius, and encouraged him to write more. It wasn't until he went to the neighboring city for high school that he found out that only sissies wrote poetry, and by then he was already a poet, a grown-up child, and unalterably ill-suited for a normal workplace.

Most are caught earlier and bent to live in the world that you and I live in, a world where their talents are taken for granted, their flaws held up for inspection. From mothers' arms to being expendable pawns in an anonymous army. From the shelter of an all-powerful father to a world where poverty waits six weeks after the pink slip.

I sat in the Mariner restaurant out in Mendota one working day, having lunch with my business friends next to a table reserved for seven. We could see the seven women at the host's stand when one of my friends idly inquired what kind of group they might be. I told him that they were housewives. Once they were seated, their conversation proved me right. I had not needed a crystal ball. Their feelings were showing on their faces. A businesswoman would not allow herself that.

I have not seen a man over ten with a naked face. Instead I have seen eyes wary of further pain, mouths controlled to elicit the desired response, necks tense with the burden of artifice, minds carefully editing the heart. These I see daily, starting with the face I see in the mirror.

Some faces are more open than others, because some people are braver than others, some safe in positions of power, and some secure in the knowledge that they are not going anywhere anyway. Some organizations are more open than others. It seems to me that the more one is measured and measurable by success in the marketplace, the more openness is valued. The more one is measured only by the perception of competence, the more the need is felt for the repression of feeling.

I think of the children. Many of us are concerned about leaving a debtor nation to our children, as well as a garbaged and depleted environment. Yet we are willing to tolerate business practices that cause us pain. We can live like this. We know we can. We have.

But think of the children. Do you want your son or daughter to live in your corporation? To be shaped by it? To have the feelings that you have? If you answer yes, I am happy for you and the environment in which you work. If you answer no, perhaps it is time to stop suffering in silence.

I have a faded and brief memory of my second day of

school. On my first day my mother walked me to school and back over what seemed an infinite and complicated distance. My second day I was to make it on my own. I have been told this. I don't remember it. My memory is of that second trip, looking over my shoulder to map for myself the way home and thinking that I saw my father a block away darting from the sidewalk to behind the line of boulevard elms. My mother confirmed years later that he had followed me to be sure that my first trip into independence ended successfully. He was amused at the number of times he had to dive for the bushes to avoid detection by the anxious and careful little boy a block ahead.

That is a faded and brief but very happy memory of
going to school. What is sad,
is that I don't remember,
ever,
coming home.

ABOUT THE AUTHOR

JOHN COWAN WAS BORN IN 1935, FILLED WITH THE OPTImism of his Swedish mother's relatives who were sure that things would come out right because they did not plan to quit until they did, and deeply influenced by his father's Irish heritage whose message was that you can go farther and faster by thinking than by sweating. Reared a Roman Catholic, he entered the monastic enclosure of a seminary as a freshman in high school (which explains why he understands classical literature and does not understand women) and stayed there through college and four years of postgraduate work, including training to be a teacher (which explains why he understands teaching and does not understand how to make money). Ordained in 1961, he was a parish priest and teacher, retreat master, preacher, and one of the founders of the priest senate in the archdiocese of Saint Paul and Minneapolis. After a while he found life a little too predictable, noticing in himself an impending sourness mixed with incipient arrogance. He required another human to remind him that he was not even important, and he needed children. In 1969, several years after most of his contemporaries, he entered the meat grinder of the pay-for-performance world. It was a shock.

Honeywell took him into the Ordinance Division, trained him in organization-development technology (training begun in the church), and allowed him to experiment by codeveloping and running the Honeywell Leadership Laboratory and a number of team-oriented projects. In 1971 he joined Dick Byrd for a roller-coaster ride of OD consulting projects, many with the federal government, several with Honeywell, and including a long-term relationship with Weyerhauser. He continued working as an independent consultant from 1974 until 1977, when he decided he was not a good enough salesman to survive. He wrote a book on management, *The Self Reliant Manager,* and sought the safe haven of a large company, Control Data. He was extraordinarily happy there for seven years, particularly during the period he was responsible for productivity education. Then for two years he was pretty miserable, put on park, waiting to be fired as Control Data began its retrenchment.

In 1985 he became an independent consultant again and discovered that somewhere along the way he had found out how to sell. He has about ten active clients, mostly in business, writes a newsletter for the fun of it, visits his friends in the trade, owns a sailboat, and makes a decent living. His wife, Edith Meissner, is a much better person than he is, and his two sons are much more impressive than he, destined to make their father look like a piker, which is exactly how he wants it.

For information on Mr. Cowan's consulting services, workshops, or newsletter, write to:

John Cowan
1498 Goodrich
St. Paul, MN 55105